Faithbuilders Bible Studies

The Prophet of Messiah

The Book of Zechariah

by Mathew Bartlett

Zechariah: Prophet of Messiah. A Study of the Book of Zechariah by Mathew Bartlett & Derek Williams

First Published in Great Britain in 2015

FAITHBUILDERS PUBLISHING www.biblestudiesonline.org.uk

An Imprint of Apostolos Publishing Ltd,
3rd Floor, 207 Regent Street,
London W1B 3HH
www.apostolos-publishing.com

Copyright © 2015 Mathew Bartlett & Derek Williams.

All rights reserved. No part of this book may be reproduced or transmitted in any form or by any means, electronic or mechanical, including photocopying, recording, or by any information storage and retrieval system, without permission in writing from the publisher.

Unless otherwise indicated, the Scripture quotations contained are from the NET Bible® copyright ©1996-2006 by Biblical Studies Press, L.L.C. http://bible.org Used by permission. All rights reserved.

Scripture quotations marked "NKJV" are taken from the New King James Version®. Copyright © 1982 by Thomas Nelson, Inc. Used by permission. All rights reserved.

British Library Cataloguing-in-Publication Data

A catalogue record for this book is available from the British Library

ISBN: 978-1-910942-10-9

Cover Design by Blitz Media, Pontypool, Torfaen

Cover Image © Dream | Dreamstime Stock Photos

First printed in Great Britain

Dedicated to all those who are hungry for God's Word.

More from Faithbuilders Bible Studies

Faithbuilders Bible studies: Matthew

Faithbuilders Bible studies: Mark

Esther – Queen of Persia

The Prophecy of Amos – A Warning for Today

Contents

Chapter 1 .... **8**
    Introduction: The Setting of the Prophet's Ministry 8
    First Vision: The Four Horses vv. 8–17 11
    Vision Two: The Four Horns vv. 18–21 15
    Discussion Questions for Chapter 1 16

Chapter 2 .... **17**
    Vision Three: The Man with a Measuring Line vv. 1–5 17
    Time to Return vv. 6–13 19
    Discussion Questions for Chapter 2 23

Chapter 3 .... **24**
    Vision Four: The Cleansing of the High Priest vv. 1–7 24
    The Greater High Priest to Come vv. 8–10 27
    Discussion Questions for Chapter 3 29

Chapter 4 .... **30**
    Vision Five: The Golden Lampstand vv. 1–6 & 11–14 30
    The Finishing of the Temple vv. 7–10 33
    Discussion Questions for Chapter 4 36

Chapter 5 .... **37**
    Introduction 37
    Vision Six: The Flying Scroll vv. 1–4 37
    Vision Seven: The Woman in the Basket vv. 5–11 39

Discussion Questions for Chapter 5 43

Chapter 6 44

Vision 8: The Vision of Four Chariots vv. 1–8 44

The Coming Priest-King vv. 9–15 47

Discussion Questions for Chapter 6 50

Chapter 7 51

Seeking God vv. 1–3 51

God's Reply vv. 4–6 52

God's Requirements vv. 7–10 52

A Warning from Israel's History vv.11–14 56

Discussion Questions for Chapter 7 57

Chapter 8 58

God's Love Motivates His Actions vv. 1–2 58

God's Sovereignty will Fulfil His Purposes vv. 3–8 59

Obedience Brings Blessing vv. 9–15 61

Ethical Responsibilities vv. 16–17 64

Forget the Former Things vv. 18–19 64

A Future Ingathering of All Nations vv. 20–32 65

Discussion Questions for Chapter 8 66

Chapter 9 67

Introduction to Chapters 9–14 67

Prophecies Against Israel's Enemies 67

The Lord Defends His People 70

The Coming King and His Reign of Abundance and Peace 71

Discussion Questions for Chapter 9 75

Chapter 10 76

The Abundant Blessing of the Lord 76

God as the Good Shepherd 76

Rejoicing in God's Victory 79

Discussion Questions for Chapter 10 82

Chapter 11 83

The Mighty will be Humbled 83

The Rejection of the Good Shepherd 84

Discussion Questions for Chapter 11 90

Chapter 12 91

God's End-Time Dealings with all Nations 91

God's End-Time Dealings with Israel 94

Discussion Questions for Chapter 12 96

Chapter 13 97

The Shepherd of My People: 97

Sin Forgiven 97

Sin Forsaken 98

Sin Frustrated 99

Discussion Questions for Chapter 13 102

Chapter 14 103

The Day of the Lord 103

The Lord is Coming to Jerusalem 106
God's Enemies Defeated 111
The Feast of Tabernacles 112
Discussion Questions for Chapter 14 115
Bibliography **116**

Chapter 1

Introduction: The Setting of the Prophet's Ministry

1:1 In the eighth month of Darius' second year, the word of the LORD came to the prophet Zechariah, son of Berechiah son of Iddo, as follows:

The inspired historian who wrote down Zechariah's prophecies dates his ministry as beginning during the reign of Darius of Persia (522-482 B.C.E),[1] meaning that Zechariah (like Haggai) began at the time when the Jews had already begun their return from exile in Babylon and were rebuilding the temple in Jerusalem.

Zechariah was a prophet who heard directly the word of the Lord; his family line is noted in order to emphasise that, like Ezekiel, he was a priest as well as a prophet.[2] It appears that his relationship with the other religious leaders started off well, although by the end of his ministry the people had become hard-hearted and the challenges of this man of God were too much for them; Jesus later spoke of Zechariah's martyrdom at their hands (Matt. 23:35).

There is a good deal of debate among scholars as to whether Zechariah is a literary unity, or whether it is actually two separate books, written by different prophets at different times.[3] For the purposes of this study, we will treat the book as being essentially one,

---

[1] Marvin A. Sweeney, *The Twelve Prophets* (Collegeville: Liturgical Press, 2001), p. 561
[2] Sweeney, p. 562
[3] James A. Hartle, "The Literary Unity of Zechariah", *The Journal of the Evangelical Theological Society* 35/2 (June 1992), pp. 145–157

with the prophecies from chapters 9–14 containing earlier material utilised by Zechariah and moulded by him to illustrate his contemporary God-given message to the exiles. Yet although the larger portion of the message was relevant to the Jews at the time of their return from exile, we shall find that many of the lessons expressed endure in their relevance to all believers throughout all time.

> 1:2 The LORD was very angry with your ancestors.

The questions of 'Why have we been in exile?' and, 'What is this return to Israel all about?' must have been important to those returning from Babylon; especially since there were very few left alive who had ever seen Israel at all, or who could remember the former temple and their previous way of life in Jerusalem. 'Why did our ancestors leave Israel, and why are we returning now?' was a hot topic. A political answer might have been, 'because Nebuchadnezzar conquered our country and took us as his slaves'; but Zechariah wants to underline the moral and spiritual reasons which lay behind these world-changing events.

Zechariah's instruction of the exiles began with reference to the sovereignty of God. It was not simply because of the geo-political situation that the Jews had been exiled. God became very angry with their ancestors because of their sin and caused them to fall into the hand of their enemies who carried them off as slaves. Their turning from God had caused him to cast them out of the land they were living in.

To a Jew, the favour of God and the blessing of living in the Promised Land were inseparable ideas. Their national identity rested largely on this: that God had brought them out of slavery in Egypt to be his people, and had given them the land to live in. Consequently a removal from the land was seen as a symbol of God's anger, whilst returning to the land was a sign of his gracious favour.

> *1:3 Therefore say to the people: The LORD who rules over all says, "Turn to me," says the LORD who rules over all, "and I will turn to you," says the LORD who rules over all.*

So Zechariah next urges the younger generation not to repeat the mistakes of the past. 'Turn to me', says God through Zechariah's message, 'and I will turn to you'. By implication God's turning to them again meant a restoration of blessing in terms of their national identity and dignity. This would involve the restoration of national worship and, in particular, the rebuilding of the temple as the focal point for that worship.

> *1:4 "Do not be like your ancestors, to whom the former prophets called out, saying, 'The LORD who rules over all says, "Turn now from your evil wickedness,"' but they would by no means obey me," says the LORD.*

Even in such a day of grace, Zechariah found it necessary to warn the returning exiles not to be stubborn and heard-hearted as their ancestors had been; who refused to hear and obey the voice of God through the former prophets. Such a warning always remains poignant, and believers today are similarly cautioned not to follow the examples of unbelief witnessed among God's people in history, but to readily hear and heed the voice of God (Heb. 3:7–8).

> *1:5-6 "As for your ancestors, where are they? And did the prophets live forever? But have my words and statutes,*

> which I commanded my servants the prophets, not outlived your fathers? Then they paid attention and confessed, 'The LORD who rules over all has indeed done what he said he would do to us, because of our sinful ways.' "

What profit did Israel make by refusing to heed God's voice? Although they rebelled against the word of God, his word stood fast and came to pass, whilst they were taken away in judgment.

The word of God outlived their ancestors. It always will. No word of God can ever fall to the ground; it must accomplish the purpose for which it was sent (Isa. 55:11). Jesus said 'My words shall never pass away' (Matt. 24:35). In view of this, an abiding principle becomes clear: it is forever unwise to ignore or disobey the word of God.

> 1:7 On the twenty-fourth day of the eleventh month, the month Shebat, in Darius' second year, the word of the LORD came to the prophet Zechariah son of Berechiah son of Iddo, as follows:

A large portion of the revelation God gave to Zechariah came in the form of dreams or visions which had meanings relevant to the people that he was ministering to. The first two of these are described in this chapter.

First Vision: The Four Horses vv. 8-17

> 1:8–10 I was attentive that night and saw a man seated on a red horse that stood among some myrtle trees in the ravine. Behind him were red, sorrel, and white horses. Then I asked one nearby, "What are these, sir?" The angelic messenger who replied to me said, "I will show

> *you what these are." Then the man standing among the myrtle trees spoke up and said, "These are the ones whom the LORD has sent to walk about on the earth."*

The vision of the four horses ought not to be confused with John's later vision of the four horsemen of the apocalypse in Revelation 6:1–8, for these riders have no sinister intent. They are servants, possibly angels, who had been sent by the Lord on a reconnaissance mission to report on the state of the earth. We may not know whether God actually does send angels to report on human affairs, or whether their presence in the vision is symbolic of God knowing completely the affairs of the world. In either case the vision speaks of God's complete and perfect knowledge of world events. Those returning from exile needed to be aware that everything which was happening was known to God and was ultimately in his hands. God always has a plan and a purpose, and Zechariah's vision shows that he was about to bring that plan to pass for the sake of the exiles of Judah.

> *1:11 The riders then agreed with the angel of the LORD, who was standing among the myrtle trees, "We have been walking about on the earth, and now everything is at rest and quiet."*

The report given by the riders was that everything on earth was at rest and quiet. Why was this information passed on to the exiles through Zechariah? Were they fearful of attack and invasion by hostile foreign powers? The word of God indicated that no such attacks were imminent or likely, and this must have reassured them to continue the work of rebuilding without fear. God had decreed a time of peace, so that his temple might be rebuilt. This is the reason why Christians are urged to pray for all in authority, so that we too might enjoy a similar time of peace in which we might live godly lives without fear (1 Tim. 2:1–3).

> *1:12–13 The angel of the LORD then asked, "LORD who rules over all, how long before you have compassion on Jerusalem and the other cities of Judah which you have been so angry with for these seventy years?" The LORD then addressed good, comforting words to the angelic messenger who was speaking to me.*

Again, it was not for the angel's benefit that this question was asked or answered; it was so that the people to whom Zechariah was ministering might know the answer. God had already said that the exile would last seventy years (Jer. 29:10). Daniel came to understand this (Dan. 9:2); and Zechariah's vision indicated that this period of time had at last been fulfilled. The return of the exiles to Jerusalem was neither the result of their own impulse, nor of a political decision by the earlier king Cyrus—it was the result of God's own plan being carried out by his wisdom and mighty power. The words of assurance given to the angel indicated that God would be with his people to help and strengthen them. God's promises through the earlier prophets would be fulfilled: the temple and the city would be rebuilt and the people would dwell in safety, walking in God's laws.

More than that, if they only knew, the time was coming near for the Messiah to be born, and he would be born in one of those cities of Judah which was being rebuilt near Jerusalem; a place called Bethlehem.

> *1:14 Turning to me, the messenger then said, "Cry out that the LORD who rules over all says, 'I am very much moved for Jerusalem and for Zion.*

Whilst the vision contains symbolic elements, there are also clear utterances concerning God's relationship with his people, such as the words here: 'I am moved for Jerusalem and for Zion.'

> *1:15 But I am greatly displeased with the nations that take my grace for granted. I was a little displeased with them, but they have only made things worse for themselves.*

At the time of the exile, God had determined to punish the nation for its idolatry and disobedience; but the nations whom he had sent to execute this punishment had gone too far in their anger. God had sought to only punish his people, but Israel's enemies sought to destroy them. The prophet hereby reveals that it was never God's intention to destroy Israel.

> *1:16 "'Therefore,' says the LORD, 'I have become compassionate toward Jerusalem and will rebuild my temple in it, 'says the LORD who rules over all.' Once more a surveyor's measuring line will be stretched out over Jerusalem.'*

God's love is always greater than his anger. Though he had punished Israel, he had not forsaken her or turned away from her completely. He reassured the exiles that he would personally see to the rebuilding of his temple. They would be his helpers in the work; surveyors and builders to work with him; but the rebuilding would be accomplished according to the immutable purpose of God.

> *1:17 Speak up again with the message of the LORD who rules over all: 'My cities will once more overflow with prosperity, and once more the LORD will comfort Zion and validate his choice of Jerusalem.' "*

God wanted the people to know that when the city and its temple were rebuilt, his blessing and their resulting prosperity would be overflowing. It would be a time of abundant blessing, in which God would once again make known to all nations that he had chosen Jerusalem as his dwelling and Israel as his people.

Vision Two: The Four Horns vv. 18-21

> *1:18–19 (2:1) Once again I looked and this time I saw four horns. So I asked the angelic messenger who spoke with me, "What are these?" He replied, "These are the horns that have scattered Judah, Israel, and Jerusalem."*

The vision has now changed. Zechariah saw four horns – always symbolic of military rulers. It was true that military rulers had scattered Israel and Judah and Jerusalem. Four great empires had ruled over them since the dispersion: the Assyrians, the Babylonians, the Medes, and now the Persians.

> *1:20–21 Next the LORD showed me four blacksmiths. I asked, "What are these going to do?" He answered, "These horns are the ones that have scattered Judah so that there is no one to be seen. But the blacksmiths have come to terrify Judah's enemies and cut off the horns of the nations that have thrust themselves against the land of Judah in order to scatter its people."*

But although men had scattered the people of Israel, God was already in the process of gathering them together again. Blacksmiths are not soldiers but craftsmen; and it was not military might that would restore Jerusalem. It was by the act of rebuilding that the nation would become a terror to its previous enemies. For when they saw what God had done for Israel, they realised that God was again among his people (Neh. 6:16), and so they were dissuaded from attacking Jerusalem.

Israel at this time remained part of the Persian Empire, an empire later taken over by Alexander the Great. Alexander's armies never actually fought in Palestine; the 'possession' of Israel merely passed to him when he defeated the Persians, at which time Jerusalem paid him tribute. So following the return from exile, there was to be no more scattering of Israel until the Romans in AD 70, nearly 600 years later.

Discussion Questions for Chapter 1

1. In what ways do you think that it was important for God to send a message of encouragement to his people through Zechariah? Why do you think such a message begins with a warning not to follow the example of previous generations?

2. Choose one of the ways in which God is described in this opening prophecy, and discuss it.

3. In what ways do you think the message of Zechariah 1 might challenge believers today?

Chapter 2

Vision Three: The Man with a Measuring Line vv. 1-5

> *2:1–3 I looked again, and there was a man with a measuring line in his hand. I asked, "Where are you going?" He replied, "To measure Jerusalem in order to determine its width and its length." At this point the angelic messenger who spoke to me went out, and another messenger came to meet him*

At the end of chapter one we saw the craftsmen coming to rebuild Jerusalem, and God promising that Judah's enemies would be thwarted in their attempts to stop the work. The same vision continues with Zechariah being shown a man approaching Jerusalem—once again like a builder—with a measuring line in his hand. His purpose was to determine Jerusalem's measurements, for from the human point of view, such things are necessary for rebuilding.

> *2:4 (NRSV) and said to him, "Run, say to that young man: Jerusalem shall be inhabited like villages without walls, because of the multitude of people and animals in it.*

Yet God intervenes in the vision, promising that ultimately human measurements would be unnecessary; God assures the people that he will sovereignly oversee the rebuilding of Jerusalem and the re-founding of the nation of Israel. This message is conveyed in the vision by means of a second angel announcing this to the first. God's message is announced to the man with the measuring line so that

Zechariah might hear and relay to the people that 'Jerusalem shall be like a city without walls'.

This statement was not intended to indicate that the walls of the city were not to be literally built (for we know that they were eventually built later under the supervision of Nehemiah), nor that measuring lines ought not to be used in their building; rather the message signified that God's blessing would overflow the city. So many people would come to dwell there during this period of peace that multitudes would dwell outside the city wall, and still be considered residents of Jerusalem. Walls could not contain the Jerusalem that God would build.

Later history indicates that this promise was not fulfilled at once. Did this suggest a lack of faith and urgency in the hearts of the people, or was God, through Zechariah, presenting the 'long view'? More than a generation later, Nehemiah was governor of a much smaller population than that which was promised here. But it has been suggested that by Jesus' time, Jerusalem was truly overflowing, especially with pilgrims on holy days.[4]

> 2:5 But I (the LORD says) will be a wall of fire surrounding Jerusalem and the source of glory in her midst.' "

Here is the reason why Jerusalem would be regarded as a city without walls—for the walls themselves would not be the city's principal means of defence. It would be the LORD who would protect the city, and he assures the returning exiles that his presence would be a wall

---

[4] Joyce C. Baldwin, *Haggai, Zechariah and Malachi* (Leicester: Tyndale, 1972), p. 106

of fire shielding them within and deterring their enemies without; his presence dwelling among them would be their glory.

This language is reminiscent of the Exodus, for when God brought Israel out of Egypt he sent a pillar of fire by day to defend his people. The implication is that in spite of all that had happened prior to the exile, the covenant which God had made with them still stood. In fact, the exile was a sign of God's keeping his covenant of love, not a sign of his annulling that covenant (Deut. 28:64). Similarly, as the people returned from exile, they could expect God to remember his covenant, giving them back their home in the Promised Land. It would be like a second Exodus.

Time to Return vv. 6–13

> *2:6–8 "You there! Flee from the northland!" says the LORD, "for like the four winds of heaven I have scattered you," says the LORD. "Escape, Zion, you who live among the Babylonians!" For the LORD who rules over all says to me that for his own glory he has sent me to the nations that plundered you -- for anyone who touches you touches the pupil of his eye.[5]*

As we saw in chapter one, it was the Lord who had scattered the nation of Israel because of their sins. The first three visions being ended, Zechariah calls on the people of Israel to return to God and to the land. Not least because at the same time that God was rebuilding the nation of Israel, he would judge the lands to which they had been taken captive. The safest place for God's people is always in the centre

---

[5] Many see vv. 6–13 as poetry, with Moffatt setting it out in stanzas; see Baldwin, p. 107

of his will, and for the Israel of Zechariah's day that meant 'return to Zion!'

It was for the sake of his own glory[6] that God would bring Israel back into their land. He did not want the nations who took them away captive to think that this had been achieved by their own might; it was *his* doing. God's dealings with his people were no business of the heathen then, and they are not today. We can have nothing in common with unbelievers. God's people were then, as they still are today, the apple of his eye (Deut. 32:10). Those who touch them (in the sense of doing evil to them) can expect retribution; and this is what is being promised here (see Rom. 12:19).

> 2:9 "I am about to punish them in such a way," he says, "that they will be looted by their own slaves." Then you will know that the LORD who rules over all has sent me.

God would punish the Babylonians by raising up against them those who had formerly been subject to them. The nations which had once been vassals of Babylon would become its masters. This could be a reference to the way that the reign of the Persians had changed the Jew's status—they were no longer slaves since Cyrus had decreed their return to Judah. The LORD God had revealed himself in all of these events to be sovereign: everything that was happening on the world stage was his doing.

> 2:10 "Sing out and be happy, Zion my daughter! For look, I have come; I will settle in your midst," says the LORD.

---

[6] 'After glory he sent me' is notoriously difficult to translate. It can mean 'after glory' or 'with glory'. But I have adopted the NET which seems to fit the context better.

This teaching that God is sovereign and immutable in his purpose should have caused rejoicing among his people; for God's purpose is ever to bless his own. God had redeemed them and would now show his blessing by dwelling among them. To the Jew, this may have been taken as a sign that God would once again establish the temple at Jerusalem; the centre of religious life and the 'dwelling' of the uncontainable God (2 Chron. 6:18).

> *2:11 "Many nations will join themselves to the LORD on the day of salvation, and they will also be my people. Indeed, I will settle in the midst of you all." Then you will know that the LORD who rules over all has sent me to you.*

God had earlier given this promise to Israel in Leviticus 26:12, and he still wishes to dwell among his people, including both Jews and Gentiles, who belong to his church today (see 2 Corinthians 6:14–18).

The messages of the prophets gave frequent glimpses of a future day in which God's blessing to Israel would overflow to reach the whole world. When this day of salvation was announced, many non-Jews would be added to the number of God's people, and God's promise was to dwell among them without making any distinction between Jew and Gentile. Even the early church found this difficult to understand (Acts 10:34-35; Acts 11:18). Yet when God speaks of nations joining themselves to Him, this implies vast numbers of Gentiles turning to God (Rev. 7:9).

> *2:12 The LORD will take possession of Judah as his portion in the holy land and he will choose Jerusalem once again.*

The message that God would include the Gentiles in his plan of salvation ought not to make anyone suppose that he had therefore rejected the Jews as his people. This message was originally given to encourage the people as they returned to Judah to start again as a nation. Israel would be his people living in his land and he would again 'choose' Jerusalem—that is, his presence would abide there; and wherever he is becomes holy (Exodus 3:5).

It is true that today the Lord has chosen his church, redeemed by his blood, to be the place in which he will dwell forever by his spirit (Eph. 2:22). Yet part of the New Testament's message is that Israel has not been rejected; in a future day they will be restored to God in a way which is very reminiscent of their restoration in the time of Zechariah (Rom. 11:26).

> *2:13 Be silent in the LORD's presence, all people everywhere, for he is being moved to action in his holy dwelling place.*

The message of Zechariah's opening two chapters has been consistent: God is sovereign. If in any way he had been thought to be inactive whilst his people were in exile, he had now acted in such a way that all nations could clearly observe what he was doing in the holy land. The wisest response of the nations was to watch God's work with silent awe and stillness; for once the Lord has begun to do a thing, it is futile for anyone to try to stop him.

The message of Zechariah was given to the exiles as they faced times of difficulty and uncertainty; albeit those difficulties were concurrent with a time of emerging national and spiritual renewal. When confronted with times of difficulty or uncertainty, a similar exhortation is suitable for Christian believers.

We have often found God's mercies to be mingled with our sorrows—and have learned that these are not contrary one to the other. And we know that God is working his purpose out for his church and for each of us individually (Rom. 8:28), knowing what is best for our eternal benefit. There are times for us, too, to be reminded to remain still and silent, leaving ourselves in the hands of a sovereign, loving and covenant-keeping God (1 Pet. 4:19).

Discussion Questions for Chapter 2

1. vv. 1–5. Why might God's covenant faithfulness to Israel give the Christian re-assurance and hope?

2. vv. 6–13. Describe what God does to demonstrate that his people are 'the apple of his eye'?

3. vv. 6–13. In what ways could you use this message to comfort God's people in times of trouble?

Chapter 3

Vision Four: The Cleansing of the High Priest vv. 1–7

> *3:1 Next I saw Joshua the high priest standing before the angel of the LORD, with Satan standing at his right hand to accuse him.*

Joshua the high priest was among those who had returned from exile in Babylon to Jerusalem. Zechariah sees him in vision form standing before the angel of the Lord with Satan making accusations against him. The devil had done the same to God's servant Job (Job 1:6–12), and presumably does so to all God's servants, since he is known as 'the accuser of the brothers' (Rev. 12:10).

> *3:2 The LORD said to Satan, "May the LORD rebuke you, Satan! May the LORD, who has chosen Jerusalem, rebuke you! Isn't this man like a burning stick snatched from the fire?"*

Joshua stands in front of the Lord as one who is justified in his sight, and so the Lord rebukes Satan for daring to bring an accusation against God's servant (Rom. 8:33); for if God be for us, who can be against us (Rom. 8:29–31)?

> *3:3 Now Joshua was dressed in filthy clothes as he stood there before the angel.*

The dirty clothes which Joshua wore were symbolic of his own sin and possibly (since the high priest represented the nation) that of all Israel. The scripture had already declared all people to be sinners, and that all human righteousness is as filthy rags (Isa. 64:6).

3:4–5 The angel spoke up to those standing all around, "Remove his filthy clothes." Then he said to Joshua, "I have freely forgiven your iniquity and will dress you in fine clothing." Then I spoke up, "Let a clean turban be put on his head." So they put a clean turban on his head and clothed him, while the angel of the LORD stood nearby.

But in a picture of cleansing, forgiveness and justification, the angel ordered Joshua's soiled clothes to be removed and that he be clothed instead with clean robes. Joshua also received a clean turban, the sign of high priestly office, which bore a gold plate engraved with the words HOLINESS TO THE LORD (Exod. 29:6; 39:30).

For the Jews, this would have been an indication that God would honour his covenant. The sin of the people was to be removed, and they would once again be seen as the nation which belonged to God, with a renewed and cleansed priesthood and a rebuilt temple. Their enemies, represented in the vision by Satan, would be unable to overcome them or thwart God's purposes.

The early church realised that this vision provided an illustration of what Christ has done for Christian believers. Christ has carried our sin away in his own body on the cross (1 Pet. 2:24) so that our filthy garments might be taken away and our sins are forgiven (1 Jn. 2:12). Subsequently, Christ clothed us with the garments of his righteousness and salvation (Isa. 61:10). By faith in Christ we are justified in God's sight (Gal. 2:16); that is, we are accepted as part of God's covenant people, in a right relationship with God. Christ has cleansed us in order to make us holy; we are a kingdom of priests (1 Pet. 2:9; Rev. 1:6) that we might serve God acceptably with reverence and godly fear (Heb. 12:28) offering spiritual sacrifices to the Lord (1 Pet. 2:5).

> *3:6–7 Then the angel of the LORD exhorted Joshua solemnly: "The LORD who rules over all says, 'If you live and work according to my requirements, you will be able to preside over my temple and attend to my courtyards, and I will allow you to come and go among these others who are standing by you.*

Having cleansed and justified Joshua, the Lord next gave him a solemn commission. The Lord's charge to Joshua was for him to perform the duties of high priest, the vision thereby ordained Joshua as high priest in the eyes of the people.

But more than that; for the return of the nation of Israel to the Promised Land was a re-establishing of their God-given call to be witnesses to the nations; and this was to be inaugurated by the consecration of their high priest as much as by the rebuilding of the temple.

Having been made holy, Joshua was to serve God in holiness of life, keeping his commandments blamelessly. This is always to be the result of consecration to God's service. Like Joshua, it is only once we have been cleansed that we can be consecrated to serve the Lord; just as in Exodus 29:20 Aaron and his sons had to have the blood of the sacrifice applied to them before they could minister. The result of our cleansing and consecration will be obedience (Rom. 6:1–2); for the deeper our appreciation of our forgiveness, the deeper will be our devotion to God (Luke 7:47).

The Greater High Priest to Come vv. 8–10

> *3:8 Listen now, Joshua the high priest, both you and your colleagues who are sitting before you, all of you are a symbol that I am about to introduce my servant, the Branch.*

God sends a message to Joshua and his contemporaries about the servant of God who was one day to appear, whom Isaiah and Jeremiah had already identified as 'the Branch' (Isa. 11:1 and Jer. 23:5). It was important to note that this Branch was to be of the line of David; yet Joshua the high priest is set forth as a picture of him in order to indicate that he would also be a priest, bearing the sin of many (Isa. 53:10–11). Of course, Israel knew that this could never be—priests only came from the tribe of Levi; yet as the writer to the Hebrews explains, the priest spoken of was appointed after the order of Melchizedek, not the order of Aaron; that is, according to the power of an endless life. Jesus Christ is the Branch born of the seed of David, who because of his endless life remains a priest of God forever (Rev. 1:18; Heb. 6:20).

> *3:9 As for the stone I have set before Joshua -- on the one stone there are seven eyes. I am about to engrave an inscription on it,' says the LORD who rules over all, 'to the effect that I will remove the iniquity of this land in a single day.*

It is uncertain whether an actual engraved precious stone was placed before Joshua during his consecration; at least in this vision of his consecration. If so, it would have served as a perpetual reminder before the people of God's promise in this verse—to remove the sin of the people through the ministry of 'the Branch'.

The Lord Jesus Christ is again and again referred to as a 'stone' in the scriptures. He is a chosen and precious stone (1 Pet. 2:4), yet he is the stone which the builders rejected (Ps. 118:22; Acts 4:11) and the one who became a trap and snare to those who did not believe (Isa. 8:14; 1 Pet. 2:7). On this stone, the Lord says, are seven eyes (originally, possibly seven facets),[7] a symbol speaking of the all-knowledge of God. The servant who is anointed with the sevenfold Holy Spirit (Rev. 4:5; Isa. 11:2) will also possess such all-knowledge. Engraved on the stone, which is Christ, is the sign that God would remove the iniquity of the people in a single day—the dreadful day when Christ hung on a cross at a place called Calvary and God laid on him the iniquity of us all (Isa. 53:6).

> 3:10 In that day,' says the LORD who rules over all, 'everyone will invite his friend to fellowship under his vine and under his fig tree.' "

The result of Christ's removing the iniquity of the people is described vividly in terms of fellowship, abundance and peace; a message which would have been welcomed by the fearful exiles. Moreover, the fact that everyone would have his own supply and could sit in peace, suggests that they would be no more slaves or servants (as had been the case in Babylon). Through Christ we enjoy fellowship with God (1 Cor. 1:9) and one another (1 Jn. 1:7). Through Christ we have peace with God (Rom. 5:1) and with each other (Eph. 2:14). Through Christ we have abundance (Rom. 8:32). Through Christ we are no longer slaves or servants but sons and friends (Gal. 3:26; Jn. 15:15).

---

[7] Baldwin, p. 116–117

Discussion Questions for Chapter 3

1. Explain how the vision of Joshua the High Priest can be used to describe what has happened to believers in Christ.

2. What should be the believer's response to being cleansed from sin by the Lord Jesus Christ?

3. vv. 8–10. In what ways might these verses provide a description of the Lord Jesus?

Chapter 4

Vision Five: The Golden Lampstand vv. 1-6 & 11-14

4:1–6 The angelic messenger who had been speaking with me then returned and woke me, as a person is wakened from sleep. He asked me, "What do you see?" I replied, "I see a menorah of pure gold with a receptacle at the top and seven lamps, with seven pipes going to the lamps. There are also two olive trees beside it, one on the right of the receptacle and the other on the left." Then I asked the messenger who spoke with me, "What are these, sir?" He replied, "Don't you know what these are?" So I responded, "No, sir." Therefore he told me, "These signify the word of the LORD to Zerubbabel: 'Not by strength and not by power, but by my Spirit,' says the LORD who rules over all."

God comes again to Zechariah through the mediation of an angel to present him with an urgent and important vision. We know it was important, for God's Word is never unimportant; yet it was also urgent, because the Lord's waking him up to give him the message denotes urgency.

In its original context the meaning of the vision was very clear to Zechariah. We must remember that Zechariah and those with him were engaged in the difficult and discouraging work of rebuilding the temple after their return from exile. Though the work of rebuilding had begun in principle some years before (in 538 BC) for various reasons it had been left unfinished and was not resumed until the time when Zechariah and Haggai prophesied to the nation.

The lampstand represented God's people on earth and their witness to the world (as did a similar lampstand in the Tabernacle – see Exodus 25:31). Just as a lamp gives light, so God's people were to bear witness to him before all people. Israel's witness was made effective through the act of rebuilding the temple, the centre of national worship. This practical work of building carried tremendous spiritual significance; for without the temple and the priesthood which accompanied it, the nation was left without a witness to the true God. As is so often the case, their faith in God was shown to be genuine by their deeds; for by their rebuilding they vowed their personal and national allegiance to the LORD.

Today, the members of Christ's church are God's people and his witnesses to the world (Acts 1:8). Jesus said that we are the light of the world (Matt. 5:14) and the book of Revelation depicts the church as a shining lampstand in a way that is reminiscent of Zechariah's vision (Rev. 1:12, 20).

The lampstand was continually fed with oil through pipes leading from a golden bowl above the lamps (working on the principle of displacement). Just as the lamps could not keep burning without the oil, so the witness of God's people could not continue without the anointing of the Holy Spirit.

In the context of Zechariah's situation, the people were weak and few and had become discouraged by the difficult work of rebuilding the temple. God was promising that the work would be completed by the help of his Spirit. In the context of the New Testament too, the Holy Spirit is the one at work in the world (Jn. 16:8-11), so that as we labour in Christ we are workers together with him (2 Cor. 6:1); he empowers and enables us by his anointing to do our part of the work.

> *4:11–14 Next I asked the messenger, "What are these two olive trees on the right and the left of the menorah?" Before he could reply I asked again, "What are these two extensions of the olive trees, which are emptying out the golden oil through the two golden pipes? He replied, "Don't you know what these are?" And I said, "No, sir." So he said, "These are the two anointed ones who stand by the Lord of the whole earth.")*

I have moved these verses for they actually refer to this section. The olive trees represented the ministry of God's servants, probably the prophets Zechariah and Haggai although it is possible that the governor Zerubbabel and priest Joshua might have been intended.

The oil in the vision was supplied *through* two trees. The branches were not the *source* of the oil; they merely carried it and poured out into the bowl on the lampstand. God's people receive the Holy Spirit from Jesus Christ himself and not through an intermediary. Nevertheless it is through the exhortation and preaching of God's word that the people of God are helped to keep their lamps trimmed and their lights burning (Matt. 25:4). This was certainly the case through Haggai and Zechariah's ministry, for as a result of their preaching the people were inspired to serve God and to reach out for more of him.

The effect of the prophets' ministry became most evident when the Jews became discouraged because of opposition, and abandoned the work of rebuilding (Ezra 4:1–5, 23–24). It was under the Spirit-anointed ministry of Zechariah and Haggai that they resumed the work (Ezra 5:1–2). Although they were a small number of people, it would not be by might of numbers that they would succeed. Solomon had employed thousands in building his temple, but God would accomplish the rebuilding of this temple with few. It would not be by power that they would accomplish the task of rebuilding; for their weakness would not hinder them. God would work in and through them by the power of his Spirit to accomplish his own purpose. The temple would be completed as God assures them in the following verses.

The Finishing of the Temple vv. 7-10

> *4:7–9 "What are you, you great mountain? Because of Zerubbabel you will become a level plain! And he will bring forth the temple capstone with shoutings of 'Grace! Grace!' because of this." Moreover, the word of the LORD came to me as follows: "The hands of Zerubbabel have laid the foundations of this temple, and his hands will complete it." Then you will know that the LORD who rules over all has sent me to you.*

If difficulties which seemed insurmountable had led to discouragement and the ceasing of the work, by the anointing of the Spirit these would be seen as nothing—for with God, the greatest obstacle is nothing. Before God's Spirit-anointed and faith-inspired people the mountains of difficulty would be removed (Mk. 11:23).

Since Haggai was bringing God's message to the people at the same time as Zechariah, knowledge of his book will help to fill the gaps in our understanding here. Having left the work because of discouragement and opposition the people began to look only after their own interests. They busied themselves with building their own houses and having what they wanted but did not give themselves to the work of God. So God sent Haggai with a message. The people repented and being encouraged, returned to the work of God wholeheartedly.

As they did so, the word of the Lord came to them again through the prophets. God said through Haggai, 'From this day I will bless you'; and through Zechariah, 'The hands of Zerubbabel have laid the foundation and his hands also shall finish it.' In other words, the temple would be completed quickly, in less than a generation, for God was working with them.

In a public ritual, Zerubbabel would bring out the symbolic finishing stone (which was not very big and usually very highly polished) and ceremonially put it in its place to officially finish and open the temple. The completion of the structure brought great rejoicing and praise and shouts of 'how beautiful it is!'

As Zechariah laid the foundation of the temple, so Jesus has laid the foundation of his church by his death and resurrection. It is on the basis of Christ's work that all who believe in Him are saved. God's people are the living stones with which God has chosen to build a living temple; a place for God to dwell with humanity. As he has begun the church, so Christ will perfect it (Heb. 12:2; Phil. 1:6). In an 'official ceremony' he will present his work to his Father (Eph. 5:27; Col 1:22). One of the purposes of the church is that it might be for the praise of God's glory forever; it is the ultimate expression of his wisdom and love. The church of Jesus Christ will offer unceasing and endless praise to God throughout all ages to come. But the church already exists, and so our work of praising and glorifying God has already begun. God has given us eternal life, so we should even now continually praise Him.

> *4:10 For who dares make light of small beginnings? These seven eyes will joyfully look on the plumb line in Zerubbabel's hand. (These are the eyes of the LORD, which constantly range across the whole earth.)*

Some might have mocked the Jews for trying to rebuild their temple, as they later mocked them for rebuilding the walls of Jerusalem. But every great project has a small beginning, and with God nothing is insignificant. The eyes of the Lord rejoiced to see the builder's tools in the hands of the king; who led the way by example, putting his shoulder to the work. Are we doing that? Are we putting ourselves entirely in the hands of God, volunteering ourselves to do whatever we can for his work?

My home church in South Wales is very small. We are physically weak with an aging congregation and we certainly have no financial muscle. Yet every day of the week we are reaching out to others with Christ's gospel and working as hard as we can for the Lord. I write this because you might be a servant of God in a similar situation: remember never to make light of small beginnings. Some time ago God gave me a vision which said that this little church in South Wales *must* stand for Jesus. I have no idea why God would see it as being strategically important, but it is so.

In American history, less than 200 men stood against a Mexican army of over 1,500 at the Alamo, Texas. A small skirmish, but one which helped change the course of the war and hence of world history. I sincerely apologise to all who dislike war for using this illustration, but it makes my point. In our holy war for truth, every small out-post of God's army is of the utmost significance in the overall battle plan of God our heavenly general. One small church may hold a place of greater significance in his plan for humankind than all the mega churches of earth. After all, it was to Bethlehem and to a life of obscurity in the small town of Nazareth that the Son of God came. Servant of God, rejoice that God's eyes, ranging over all the earth, are always focused upon you, however little you might think yourself!

Discussion Questions for Chapter 4

1. In what way was the help of God's Spirit communicated to the exiles at this time?

2. What obstacles hindered the rebuilding of the temple? Can you recognise any of these difficulties in your own service for God?

3. Discuss how God's promise 'not by might, nor by power, but by my Spirit' ought to encourage you to continue your service for God.

Chapter 5

Introduction

Although the exiles had returned from Babylon to rebuild the temple, God had still had work to do in order to make them a people worthy of such a place of worship; and worthy of the God who would be worshipped there. In their immediate context, the two visions Zechariah saw in this chapter deal with the issue of sin being purged from the land. It was not sufficient for God's people to worship him in a holy temple; the worshippers themselves were to be holy and observe God's laws. In the same way that they had been taught to purge out yeast from their homes before Passover (Ex. 12:15), so they were now to purge iniquity out of the land; and they were to begin by looking at their individual lives. Christians are similarly instructed to cleanse malice and wickedness out of their lives (1 Cor. 5:7), for we too must be a holy people to serve God (1 Pet. 2:9).

Vision Six: The Flying Scroll vv. 1–4

> *5:1–2 Then I turned to look, and there was a flying scroll! Someone asked me, "What do you see?" I replied, "I see a flying scroll thirty feet long and fifteen feet wide."*

In this vision, Zechariah saw a scroll of huge dimensions flying in the sky. This scroll was open to its full extent, presumably so that even from its aerial position everyone could read what was written on it. It may further be significant that the dimensions of the scroll match those of the porch in Solomon's temple,[8] for with the rebuilding of the

---

[8] Rex Mason, *The Books of Haggai, Zechariah and Malachi* (Cambridge: University Press, 1977), p. 57 (see 1 Kings 6:3)

temple came the renewed call for holiness and purity among God's people who would approach him to worship.

> 5:3 The speaker went on to say, "This is a curse traveling across the whole earth. For example, according to the curse whoever steals will be removed from the community; or on the other hand (according to the curse) whoever swears falsely will suffer the same fate."

Most commentators regard the scroll as representing the word of God, or at least some part of the law given by Moses. The law contained blessings for obedience and curses for disobedience (e.g. Deut. 28). If the exiles themselves failed to take action against the wicked in their midst (e.g. Deut. 13:5; 22:22) they are assured that God himself would act in this matter. Those who wronged their neighbours in any way (the word used for 'steals' is suggestive of any wrong doing) and those who wrong God (by swearing falsely or using his name in vain) would both would be cut off from the community— they were not to be counted among God's people. This declaration may well have provided an opportunity for individuals and the nation as a whole to repent before these unspecified judgments came upon them.

Ezekiel had already taught Jews the concept of individual responsibility (Ezek. 18:4), and Zechariah marries this concept to that of national purity. The purity of the whole lump is compromised by the presence of just a small batch of yeast.

In the New Testament, Christians are warned to expel from their midst those who—although professing Christ as Saviour—live in open defiance of his commands (e.g. 1 Cor. 5.1–2) and to withdraw from the company of those who are disobedient (1 Tim. 6:5; 1 Cor. 5:11; Rom. 16:17; 2 Thess. 3:6; 2 Thess. 3:14).

> *5:4 "I will send it out," says the LORD who rules over all, "and it will enter the house of the thief and of the person who swears falsely in my name. It will land in the middle of his house and destroy both timber and stones."*

Not only would evil befall the offenders who persisted in their sins, but their houses, too, would be levelled. This may literally have been enacted, but is more likely to be a metaphor for the utter calamity that they would experience. God has ways of bringing retribution throughout the world. Zechariah here calls him 'the LORD who rules over all'. There is nowhere to hide our secret sins from an all knowing God; and he is a God who will punish sin in the present life as well as in the next.

Vision Seven: The Woman in the Basket vv. 5-11

> *5:5–6 After this the angelic messenger who had been speaking to me went out and said, "Look, see what is leaving." I asked, "What is it?" And he replied, "It is a basket for measuring grain that is moving away from here." Moreover, he said, "This is their 'eye' throughout all the earth."*

The next vision is of another flying object, this time a basket of grain departing from Zechariah's position. The basket was recognised by the prophet as being an ephah, a measuring basket that was used in everyday life and also in the worship of God in the temple. Their 'eye' (NET above) is better rendered 'resemblance' (AV). The angel is about to show Zechariah something which may be observed among all the peoples of the world.

> *5:7–8 Then a round lead cover was raised up, revealing a woman sitting inside the basket. He then said, "This woman represents wickedness," and he pushed her down into the basket and placed the lead cover on top.*

The angel then lifted the cover of the ephah to show Zechariah what was inside. That this cover was made of lead may indicate that a heavy weight was required to prevent the escape of the contents. Within the basket was a woman; so either this was a very small woman or the ephah was unusually large—for usually it held between 5 and 10 gallons, and so was not large enough to hold a person. The identity of the woman was unimportant, it is what she represents that matters: wickedness or immorality. Not the iniquity of an individual or even of the nation of Israel, for the angel had already said that she represented the iniquity which is found 'in all the earth'.

> *5:9–11 Then I looked again and saw two women going forth with the wind in their wings (they had wings like those of a stork and they lifted up the basket between the earth and the sky. I asked the messenger who was speaking to me, "Where are they taking the basket?" He replied, "To build a temple for her in the land of Babylonia. When it is finished, she will be placed there in her own residence."*

Some commentators believe these verses are a depiction of God's removal of Israel's sin by his grace, but this over-simplified position is a difficult one to defend. When God removes his peoples' sins, it is 'as far as the east is from the west' (Ps. 103:12); whereas the 'iniquity' in this vision is removed only as far as Babylon. Moreover, even the Old Testament makes clear that the promise 'to remember their sins no more' is connected to the 'New Covenant'—and no new covenant is spoken of here.

It may be, however, that much of the moral filth which had affected the nation was to be removed and symbolically put back where it belonged. These Jews had lived in Babylon, the idolatrous capital of the world. The woman was taken away to a house (possibly a temple, as NET above) denoting that her idolatrous influence would be removed from the nation. The meaning then becomes plain, the people who worshiped God in the new temple in Jerusalem were to be pure worshippers of Jehovah, not idolaters—for idolatry had been the cause for their being carried captive into Babylon in the first place. It may in this connection be significant that under later reforms introduced by Nehemiah, those Jews who had married foreign wives were compelled to send them and their children away, because of their idolatrous influences. Did they return to Babylon?

In the New Testament, believers are referred to as the temple of the Living God, and are command to flee from idolatry (1 Cor. 10:14; 2 Cor. 6:16). Our worship of God today must be no less pure than that which, through Zechariah, was demanded of Israel.

It is worthy of note that the vision of the woman in the basket may have had a wider symbolic meaning, especially to the writers of the New Testament. The vision of the woman representing wickedness is used again in Revelation 17, this time to denote the sinful world system which controls people's hearts in opposition to Christ. This antichrist spirit is manifested in world politics, world religion, and even in world finance and commerce. In this regard, several New Testament writers refer to iniquity as a spirit, or a worldwide spiritual phenomenon. The secret mystery of lawlessness is already at work in the world (2 Thess. 2:7). Sin itself is a powerful controlling force in the hearts of men and women, and its power is derived – at least in part – from the satanic forces of darkness (Eph. 2:2); which are themselves in rebellion against God. Only Christ can break the hold of this evil power in individual lives (Col. 1:13).

Having been set free by Jesus, the Christian is not to become bound again by the spirit of this age. We are to avoid ungodly companionships (2 Cor. 6:14; Jas. 4:4) as John hears during one of his visions in the Book of Revelation—God's voice calling—'come out of her my people' (Rev. 18:4). The message of Zechariah to the Jews of his time is in this sense identical to the message of the Bible for Christians today, 'be holy for I am holy' (1 Pet. 1:16); separate yourselves from idolatrous influences, drawing near to God and worshipping him in his holy temple; which today is the function of the church of Christ (hence the call in 1 John 5:21 to 'keep yourselves from idols').

Since Zechariah's vision was used by New Testament writers to link into their apocalyptic visions, one further step might be tentatively taken in our understanding of this vision. In the very last days, the mystery of lawlessness will find expression in a man who will epitomise rebellion against God, submitting the allegiance of his soul entirely to Satan, and deceiving the whole world of that time to worship Satan instead of Christ. This man embodies the spirit of antichrist, and so is often referred to simply as *the antichrist*. Clearly we cannot carry the parallel too far, for the antichrist is said to rule from Jerusalem not Babylon, yet similarities are also apparent. Firstly, if the woman in Zechariah's vision was restrained by a heavy lead weight, Paul tells us that the manifestation of the man of sin will be restrained by the Holy Spirit until God's appointed time (2 Thess. 2:7). He will ultimately be destroyed, and so will the whole world's opposition to Christ, for he will come to reign as absolute ruler, with all things subjected under his feet. Moreover, Jerusalem, though not referred to as Babylon, is referred to as Egypt and Sodom in Revelation 11:8 and Isaiah 1:10. This demonstrates that the actual location of Babylon may not be as significant to the New Testament writers' understanding of this text as the unfaithfulness to God that it represents.

Discussion Questions for Chapter 5

1. In what ways are God's people called to be holy to the Lord?

2. In Zechariah's vision, what do you think the removal of iniquity from the land signified?

3. The New Testament writers appear to allude to this vision in relation to their understanding of the evil forces at work in this world. What forms can this evil take and in what way shall it ultimately be defeated?

Chapter 6

Vision 8: The Vision of Four Chariots vv. 1-8

6:1 Once more I looked, and this time I saw four chariots emerging from between two mountains of bronze.

In this eighth vision, Zechariah sees four chariots coming out from an entrance which is sided by two mountains of bronze. Since it is later explained (6:5) that the chariots are coming out of God's immediate presence, the mountains must refer symbolically to the gates of heaven, or the approach to God's high throne. It is significant that two bronze pillars sided the entrance into Solomon's temple (1 Kgs. 7:13–22). As bronze is strong, so God's presence is an impregnable fortress, a safe refuge for his people. God is far beyond every human attempt to dethrone him (Ps. 2:1–4). The mountains may represent God's immovable and immutable purpose which is behind every event on earth; emphasising the sovereignty of God in human affairs (Acts 2:23; Acts 4:28). As Matthew Henry says 'His providences move swiftly and strongly as chariots, but all directed and governed by his infinite wisdom and sovereign will, as chariots by their drivers.'

Some commentators have thought that the four chariots represent four kingdoms, but it there is little in the text to support this view.

6:2–3 Harnessed to the first chariot were red horses, to the second black horses, to the third white horses, and to the fourth spotted horses, all of them strong.

In the Book of Revelation, John has a similar vision of four horsemen riding out to accomplish God's purposes on earth in the form of war, death, famine and plague (Rev. 6:1–8). What the colours in Zechariah's somewhat different vision signify is not revealed to the prophet, but by comparison with Revelation we may observe that God employs various means to fulfil his purposes on earth, yet all these means are in his hands.

> *6:4–5 Then I asked the angelic messenger who was speaking with me, "What are these, sir?" The messenger replied, "These are the four spirits of heaven that have been presenting themselves before the Lord of all the earth.*

The chariots and their horses are symbolic of God's involvement in the affairs of people and nations. In this kind of vision, it is not necessary for us to suppose that these are literally angels or some other spiritual beings having personality. For even if God's purposes are symbolised by an army of chariots, that does not suggest that God necessarily requires human or angelic armies to accomplish his ends. Whilst God's angels are sometimes depicted as being like chariots (Ps. 68:17), such language is figurative, for God has no need to ride in a chariot—not even an angelic chariot! Just as in the previous vision, the flying scroll represented God's word, so here the chariots and horses depict God's providence. As the wind covers the whole earth (which is why four winds are mentioned: North, South, East and West) so God in his providence reigns over the entire world. God even has the wind under his control, which no man can tame. The visionary 'angels' next receive their instructions from the Lord as to what they are to do on earth.

> *6:6–8 The chariot with the black horses is going to the north country and the white ones are going after them,*

> *but the spotted ones are going to the south country. All these strong ones are scattering; they have sought permission to go and walk about over the earth." The Lord had said, "Go! Walk about over the earth!" So they are doing so. Then he cried out to me, "Look! The ones going to the northland have brought me peace about the northland."*

Whatever they had been sent out to achieve was accomplished, although details of their tasks are not given. The vision is intended to show that God's purpose will stand, since no human power is able to annul it. This revelation sets the stage for the next vision, or rather the prophetic instruction given to Zechariah; a prophecy which, whilst it may have held some significance for the exiles, pointed towards a future day.

The reference to those going north bringing peace to God may be an indication to the recent removal by God of the Babylonian power, and the installation of the more southerly Persian power, through whom God brought about the emancipation of the exiled Jews. Yet the return of the exiles from Babylon and the rebuilding of the temple was only one part of the much larger purpose of God. God's activity had not begun with the returned exiles, nor would it end with them; yet as they played their part, they were given assurance of the final fulfilment of all God's promises. That is why the exhortation of the final verse (6:15) is so important. The whole accomplishment of God's salvation history did not rest with them, just as the whole responsibility for the salvation of humankind does not rest with the church today. Nevertheless they had their responsibilities and we have ours. Jesus will indeed reign over all the earth, but his servants are accountable to proclaim him as Lord to every nation (Rom. 10:14);

just as, whilst God promised the exiles that the temple would be successfully reconstructed, he also commanded them to fetch the wood and stone with which to build (Hag. 1:8).

The Coming Priest-King vv. 9–15

> *6:9–11 The word of the LORD came to me as follows: "Choose some people from among the exiles, namely, Heldai, Tobijah, and Jedaiah, all of whom have come from Babylon, and when you have done so go to the house of Josiah son of Zephaniah. Then take some silver and gold to make a crown and set it on the head of Joshua son of Jehozadak, the high priest.*

The men named in these verses were probably respected elders who served as witnesses to Zechariah's prophetic action; this seems to be the only significance of their presence in the narrative.

The Hebrew word used for 'crown' is plural, suggesting that this is a crown of crowns (or a crown fashioned within a crown) as in Revelation 19:12.[9] What is unusual about this enacted coronation is that God commands Zechariah to place the crown on the head of the high priest and not that of the king (or governor, as he was at that time). History does not indicate that this action of Zechariah was seen as treacherous by the supporters of Zerubbabel, nor is there evidence that Joshua son of Jehozadak ever usurped the secular power. Joshua and Zerubbabel seem to have governed Judah well, side by side, within their separate secular and religious spheres. So clearly this prophecy of Zechariah was taken by the exiles to have a symbolic meaning relating to a future day.

---

[9] Baldwin, p. 133

> *6:12–13 and speak unto him, saying, Thus speaketh the LORD of hosts, saying, Behold, the man whose name is the Branch; and he shall grow up out of his place, and he shall build the temple of the LORD: even he shall build the temple of the LORD; and he shall bear the glory, and shall sit and rule upon his throne; and he shall be a priest upon his throne: and the counsel of peace shall be between them both. (RV)*

The sovereignty which was pictured in the vision at the opening of the chapter would one day be embodied in a person, whose name is 'the Branch'. The Jews already understood 'the Branch' to be a reference to the future Davidic king spoken of by Isaiah and Jeremiah (Isa. 11:1; Jer. 23:5; Jer. 33:15). Joshua (or Jeshua) is the Hebrew equivalent of Jesus; so the very name of the coming Messiah is here announced. The temple was meant to be his throne (Mal. 3:1), but being initially rejected by his own people, he has been gloriously exalted (Phil. 2:9) and has taken joint possession of God's throne (Rev. 3:21), until he returns to earth to take up the throne of David (Luke 1:32).

However, this interpretation does present a problem. For according to the Law of Moses kings of Israel could only come from the tribe of Judah, and priests only from the tribe of Levi; and so how could the idea of a king also being a priest be reconciled?

It is clear that our Lord was descended from Judah, not Levi, and so he could not ever become a priest according to the covenant which God gave to Moses. Even so, the vision suggests a future time when this problem would be settled. The writer to the Hebrews sets out to explain that Jesus was not made a priest by a regulation with regard to his ancestry, but with an oath from God that he would abide as an eternal priest after the order of Melchizedek. This change of priesthood would require the introduction of a new and better covenant (see Hebrews chapter 7). The office of king and priest would be united in the Christ (this is what the 'counsel of peace' refers to). 'The Branch' shall be invested with royal majesty; and yet as king-priest he would rise from obscurity, as a branch out of dry ground. One might have expected such a king to come from an exalted background, but Jesus was born into poverty to a lowly family from Nazareth. Nevertheless it was to Jesus of Nazareth that God entrusted the task of building a temple made without hands; consisting of men and women from every nation who would worship God in Spirit and truth (1 Cor. 3:16; John 4:20–24).

So whilst some commentators rightly depict Zerubbabel and Joshua being as one in their building of the temple and governing Jerusalem (which was indeed the case), the text is clearly signifying an even greater day of future Messianic glory.

> *6:14 The crown will then be turned over to Helem, Tobijah, Jedaiah, and Hen son of Zephaniah as a memorial in the temple of the LORD.*

The crown, once made, was to be placed in the rebuilt temple as a constant reminder before the worshippers of God's promise concerning the future Davidic king. God had previously instructed Israel to keep reminders of God's past dealings to stir them to worship; what was unusual about this crown was that provided an object lesson relating to the future.

Likewise, in the Christian memorial—the communion service—we are exhorted to look back to what the Lord Jesus did to redeem our souls on the cross; but we must also look forward, since the apostle declared that the observance of the communion would continue only 'until he comes' (1 Cor. 11:26).

> *6:15 Then those who are far away will come and build the temple of the LORD so that you may know that the LORD who rules over all has sent me to you. This will all come to pass if you completely obey the voice of the LORD your God." ' "*

The building of the temple by returning Jews was already underway. It may well have been that as the people found the rebuilding difficult, God's promise was of more exiles returning from Babylon to help in the work. Yet it may be reasonable to suggest that this this prophecy might also relate to the inclusion of Gentiles in the community of faith which the coming Davidic king would bring about; for they too would become part of that spiritual temple which Christ was to build and is still building (Eph. 3:6).

Discussion Questions for Chapter 6

1. What does the vision of the four chariots tell you about God's purposes for this world?

2. vv.9–15. Assuming that these verses may be read as a Messianic prophecy, how is the Messiah here described?

3. vv.14–15. Think again of the idea of God giving us a 'memorial of things to come'. What aspects of Jesus' promise to return fill you with hope?

Chapter 7

Seeking God vv. 1–3

> *7:1–3 In King Darius' fourth year, on the fourth day of Kislev, the ninth month, the word of the LORD came to Zechariah. Now the people of Bethel had sent Sharezer and Regem-Melech and their companions to seek the LORD's favor by asking both the priests of the temple of the LORD who rules over all and the prophets, "Should we weep in the fifth month, fasting as we have done over the years?"*

Zechariah carefully records the time when the returned exiles had sent representatives to inquire of God regarding their religious observance of fasting in the fifth month. This regular fasting had been the practice of the Jews throughout their seventy years in exile; and it may have been that since God had kept his promise to restore them to the land, they wanted to know if they ought rather to rejoice than mourn.

It does appear that God was working on these men by his Spirit, stirring them from apathy and indifference to genuinely seek the will and mind of God. It was God's moving on them in this way that caused them to challenge the status quo and re-evaluate the things they had always done; they did not wish merely to go through the motions but get serious with God. There are times when we too must awake from our apathy to seek God with all our hearts and ensure that we are in the centre of his will, doing what he requires of us.

God's Reply vv. 4-6

7:4-6 The word of the LORD who rules over all then came to me, "Speak to all the people and priests of the land as follows: 'When you fasted and lamented in the fifth and seventh months through all these seventy years, did you truly fast for me — for me, indeed? And now when you eat and drink, are you not doing so for yourselves?'"

As the prophets waited on God, God spoke through Zechariah to challenge this practice of fasting with the searching question: 'did you fast for me?' In other words, was this a genuine religious observance, or simply a matter of course? Like many traditions, this fast began with the best motives; but over time it became an empty formality.

There are times when God does call and require a fast (e.g. Joel 2:15) but always in connection with genuine repentance and turning to God, never as a meaningless ritual. Indeed, that God takes no pleasure in outward observances without inward piety had already been made clear by the prophets (e.g. Amos 5:21-22; Isa. 66:3). There is absolutely no use in our keeping up any form of religious observance if our hearts are far from God; yet God accuses Israel of doing exactly that—for whether fasting or eating their hearts were focused on themselves.

God's Requirements vv. 7-10

7:7-10 Should you not have obeyed the words that the LORD cried out through the former prophets when Jerusalem was peacefully inhabited and her surrounding cities, the Negev, and the Shephelah were also populated? Again the word of the LORD came to Zechariah: "The LORD who rules over all said, 'Exercise true judgment and

> *show brotherhood and compassion to each other. You must not oppress the widow, the orphan, the foreigner, or the poor, nor should anyone secretly plot evil against his fellow human being.'*

God's reply is very enlightening. He brings the exiles no new message, but refers them back to the messages given to their fore-fathers who had refused to listen when they lived in peace before the exile. If they had heeded God's word and obeyed his voice then they would never have been removed to Babylon.

So God restates the message given through the earlier prophets, summarising it by means of three positive and five negative commands:

Exercise true judgment. Primarily this refers to the law courts. Bribery, partiality and corruption were common before the exile (Amos 5:12; Mic. 3:11) but they were now to be things of the past in both civil and criminal courts. In a broader sense, God's words imply doing the right thing and dealing fairly in all circumstances; whether that means employers paying fair wages to employees and ensuring good working conditions, or a father providing for his family; indeed doing whatever else is just and right.

Show mercy (NET – *brotherhood*). The word used implies love and forgiveness. It is the opposite of the inhuman and unmerciful attitude of people who do not value human life or show care towards their fellow human beings. God's love is for everyone and so our love must be for our neighbour, whoever they may be. God has forgiven us so much that we are at fault if we fail to forgive others, especially those who are our Christian brothers and sisters (Matt. 18:21–22; Luke

17:3–4). Jesus several times emphasised the passage of Hosea which makes clear that God requires mercy and not sacrifice (Hos. 6:6; Matt. 9:13).

Compassion. The New Testament is very clear on this subject, that compassion is the practical expression of love (1 John 3:17). This fits with Zechariah's understanding and his view of godly fasting compares well with Isaiah's (Isa. 58:5–7). There are so many needs in our world—are we able to meet just some? If we are not moved with compassion when we see others in desperate poverty or suffering with life threatening illness, then we must question the state of our relationship with God. It would make no difference if we fasted each day for twelve months of the year, if we failed to show love and compassion (1 Cor. 13:3). The New Testament contains commands that we are to remember the poor (Gal. 2:10; Acts 20:35; Mark 14:7); just as the rest of Scripture promises many blessings to those who do (Ps. 41:1; Prov. 22:9; Prov. 28:27).

As Christians, we are members of one body—the church—and if one member of the body suffers, the whole body suffers. Hence Christians should especially remember *other Christians* in need. In the first century, the Gentile churches did so by sending offerings to their poorest brothers, the saints in Judea (Rom. 15:26); may we emulate their example.

Do not oppress widows or orphans. These groups in society were helpless in Zechariah's time. In the days before welfare or social security, if a widow and her children had no family or breadwinner for the household then they were destitute apart from the mercy of God. But God takes upon himself the task of being a father to the fatherless and a husband to the widow (Ps. 68:5). Jesus took a similar role when he rebuked Pharisees for extorting money from widows (Matt. 23:14); and in its earliest days, the church cared for believing widows who were genuinely destitute; although those with relatives were to be cared for by their families (1 Tim. 5:3, 16).

Christians can join God in his care of the vulnerable in a variety of ways. The Christian tradesperson, for example, who decides to make a little less profit than usual when working for a widow will be repaid by God; as will those who remember orphans with gifts.

Do not oppress the foreigner. There was to be no racism among God's people. They were to welcome any foreigners with open arms, remembering that they were once strangers in Egypt (Exod. 23:9). Of all people, the Jews should have realised that it is not easy to be a stranger in a strange land; and that many migrants had come to Israel to escape the evils of poverty, tyranny and idolatry. The Christian church today should be the most welcoming place for immigrants from any nation.

Do not oppress the poor. This is the negative aspect of the corresponding positive command to show compassion. The poor were desperate for work, and so would accept very little pay. Employers were not to exploit this. The poor had no recourse to payment of lawyers' fees; and so could easily be unfairly defeated in court. Yet God would remain as their righteous judge.

nor should anyone secretly plot evil against his fellow human being. Violence and malice of all kinds whether expressed in robbery, assault, or other acts inspired by jealousy or hatred are the opposite of love and are abhorrent to God. Such acts were to have no lodging place among God's restored people (Eph. 4:31–32).

A Warning from Israel's History vv.11–14

> 7:11–14 *"But they refused to pay attention, turning away stubbornly and stopping their ears so they could not hear. Indeed, they made their heart as hard as diamond, so that they could not obey the Torah and the other words the LORD who rules over all had sent by his Spirit through the former prophets. Therefore, the LORD who rules over all had poured out great wrath. " 'It then came about that just as I cried out, but they would not obey, so they will cry out, but I will not listen,' the LORD who rules over all had said. 'Rather, I will sweep them away in a storm into all the nations they are not familiar with.' Thus the land had become desolate because of them, with no one crossing through or returning, for they had made the fruitful land a waste."*

God's warning to the returned exiles is that they should listen to and obey the voice of God. They were not to do what their forefathers had done prior to the exile; for although they heard word of God, they refused to listen and hardened their hearts so as not to obey, even though they heard his words again and again (Heb. 3:15).

Whoever rejects the voice of God speaking to them puts themselves outside of God's mercy and stores up judgment for themselves; just as Israel's refusal to hear caused the destruction of their land and their being carried away into exile. Similar judgment awaits all who harden their hearts and refuse to listen to the voice of God (Heb. 3:12; Prov. 29:1; Rom. 2:5–6).

Discussion Questions for Chapter 7

1. vv.1–3. In what ways could you examine your life to ensure that you are following God's will, and not merely going through the motions?

2. vv.7–10. From these verses list several points about how you can live in the way that God requires.

3. vv.11–14. Why is it a dangerous thing for a person to harden their hearts and refuse to listen to the voice of God?

Chapter 8

Chapter 8 is a continuation of chapter 7[10] and eventually (8:19) the answer is given to the opening question about the observance of fast days. Having rehearsed why the people were taken into exile, the prophet now expounds on why they had been brought back, and what were God's intentions towards them.

God's Love Motivates His Actions vv. 1–2

8:1–2 And the word of the LORD of hosts came to me, saying, Thus saith the LORD of hosts: I am jealous for Zion with great jealousy, and I am jealous for her with great fury. (RV)

Despite having punished their fathers for their sin and wilful rejection of his message through the prophets, God remained ever mindful of his covenant with Israel (Zion), through which he had made them his own people. The underlying meanings of the words 'jealous', 'jealousy' and 'fury' carry the idea of the deep emotion or intense love by which God is motivated to act on behalf of his people. When they reject him, he is stirred to chastise them; but when they repent he is equally determined to restore and bless them. Zechariah makes clear that the blessings he is about to speak of find their root in the loving and gracious heart of God—as do all the things which happen to God's people (Rom. 8:28).

---

[10] Assis suggests that it is actually a revision and digest of chapters 1–7. Ellie Assis, "Zechariah 8 as Revision and Digest of Zechariah 1–7" *JHS* Vol. 10, Article 15

God's Sovereignty will Fulfil His Purposes vv. 3-8

> *8:3 The Lord says, 'I have returned to Zion and will live within Jerusalem. Now Jerusalem will be called "truthful city," "mountain of the LORD who rules over all," "holy mountain."'*

God asserts that he had already returned to the people, that he might once again dwell among them. They should have already realised this, since they had returned from exile in fulfilment of God's promise. Once more the city of Jerusalem, though now a ruin, would be called the faithful city; the holy place where God dwelt and where he could be worshipped (a reference to the rebuilding of the temple). When people came to the rebuilt temple at Jerusalem to humbly seek God he would be found by them.

God's promise to continue dwelling among them implies that Israel, as a result of God's mercy, would become faithful and true to his covenant; from this we understand that the spiritual as well as the national restoration of God's people is attributed to divine grace and sovereign action.

> *8:4–5 Moreover, the LORD who rules over all says, 'Old men and women will once more live in the plazas of Jerusalem, each one leaning on a cane because of advanced age. And the streets of the city will be full of boys and girls playing.*

Baldwin suggests that since many elderly people were not considered fit to travel the 3 ½ month journey from Babylon to Jerusalem there were very few of them living among the returned exiles at that time.[11] But now God would show his blessing to Israel in two ways – the old would live to a ripe age, and the streets would be filled with young children playing. The picture is of one of peace, prosperity and freedom; for the aged being unafraid to walk the streets, and the children being unhindered at play indicates the absence of anything like conflict or tyranny.

> *8:6 And, 'says the LORD who rules over all, 'though such a thing may seem to be difficult in the opinion of the small community of those days, will it also appear difficult to me?' asks the LORD who rules over all.*

For the small band of returned exiles, the idea that the city of Jerusalem would soon become full and prosperous seemed far-fetched. All around them were the ruins of the houses which had been abandoned during the Babylonian invasion. However could such devastation be restored?

But God gives his Word that it will be so. He had already revealed to Zechariah that his purposes would be accomplished, 'not by might or power but by my Spirit' (4:6). When God has purposed to do something it shall be done for, as Jeremiah says, 'Is anything too hard for the Lord?' (Jer. 32:27)

As the church of Jesus Christ in our own nation appears spiritually weak, rent by false doctrines and deceptive spiritual manifestations; and as it decreases its adherents annually to ever fewer numbers, one might think it incredible that God in his sovereignty might decide to grant repentance, revival and blessing to the whole nation; but it will

---

[11] Baldwin, p. 150

not be remarkable or too hard for God. In fact God would rather accomplish great things with minorities and nobodies than with the great and strong, for then all glory goes to him (1 Cor. 1:29).

> *8:7–8 "The LORD who rules over all asserts, 'I am about to save my people from the lands of the east and the west. And I will bring them to settle within Jerusalem. They will be my people, and I will be their God, in truth and righteousness.'*

God here indicates the way in which he will bring his purpose to pass. He will call his people to return to Israel from all parts of the earth (from sunrise to sunset) and they will settle in Jerusalem. Nor will this be merely a physical return, for the returning exiles will become true worshippers of God, returning to him with all their hearts, not falsely as their fathers had done; calling on him in truth and seeking to obey his will.

Obedience Brings Blessing vv. 9–15

> *8:9 "The LORD who rules over all also says, 'Gather strength, you who are listening to these words today from the mouths of the prophets who were there at the founding of the house of the LORD who rules over all, so that the temple might be built.*

Whilst it is true that God sovereignly does his own work, it remains important for his servants to perform theirs in cooperation with him. The people had begun to build the temple, but by inference from Haggai (Hag. 1:2–4), we see that they had temporarily stopped. Now Zechariah urges them to let their hands be strong to do the work; it is a call to action.

> *8:10 Before that time there was no compensation for man or animal, nor was there any relief from adversity for those who came and went, because I had pitted everybody — each one — against everyone else.*

It was God's Spirit who moved the people to begin the building of the house of the Lord, and as they obediently did so, God responded by blessing them. God specifies the day when the foundation of the temple was laid as the day when he began to turn their curses to blessings (Hag. 2:18–19). Until then he had robbed them of peace and brought adversity on them; but when they heeded his voice to go up and rebuild the temple he began to bless them. The application of such teaching to God's people today is evident – it is obedience which leads to blessing.

The pause in building had led to a temporary reversal in Israel's fortunes (Hag. 1:7–11), but now the prophet encourages them to persist in the work, for as they did so God would restore his blessings.

> *8:11–12 But I will be different now to this remnant of my people from the way I was in those days,' says the LORD who rules over all, 'for there will be a peaceful time of sowing, the vine will produce its fruit and the ground its yield, and the skies will rain down dew. Then I will allow the remnant of my people to possess all these things.*

Unlike during the days of exile, God's people in Judea would be blessed with peace and harmony, fruitfulness and prosperity. The picture is one of God's overflowing blessing in every area of life.

> *8:13 And it will come about that just as you (both Judah and Israel) were a curse to the nations, so I will save you*

and you will be a blessing. Do not be afraid! Instead, be strong!'

When God's wrath was upon the nation, they had been derided and cursed by all other nations; but now they would be considered blessed, for God was with them. With this encouragement they were to be strong and keep up the work without giving way to fear.

The act of worship required by God from the nation of Israel on this occasion was the rebuilding of the temple. What is your act of acceptable worship to God (Rom. 12:1)? The blessing began when they were prepared to put God first and make him the centre of their lives. It always works that way. Are you putting God first in your life; are you fully surrendered to him?

> *8:14–15 "For the LORD who rules over all says, 'As I had planned to hurt you when your fathers made me angry, 'says the LORD who rules over all, 'and I was not sorry, so, to the contrary, I have planned in these days to do good to Jerusalem and Judah — do not fear!*

God once again assures the people of his sovereignty. When the people did wrong he punished them; they were carried away into exile even when they believed such a thing could not happen. But it did happen, for God had purposed it. In the same way, since God had now purposed to restore and bless them, they were not to be afraid; for who can hinder God?

Perhaps you have recently come back to God, or at least you have decided you want to be closer to the Lord, but find it hard and fear that you will not be able to keep it up. Do not fear, for the fact you are trying to return is evidence that God has purposed to bless you and that he will help you to stand.

Ethical Responsibilities vv. 16-17

> 8:16 These are the things you must do: Speak the truth, each of you, to one another. Practice true and righteous judgment in your courts.

Once again, as in chapter seven, God reminds the people of their ethical responsibilities. God cannot punish the sins of the fathers and overlook the same sins in their descendants. The returned exiles must hear and obey the voice of God. The commands are the same as those given earlier, with the addition 'do not lie to each other' (Eph. 4:25).

> 8:17 Do not plan evil in your hearts against one another. Do not favor a false oath — these are all things that I hate,' says the LORD."

This verse reveals the basis of all Christian ethics. God's people strive to do what pleases him, and avoid certain things not simply because they are 'wrong', but because God is displeased with them. The good pleasure of God is what decides every Christian's moral compass.

Forget the Former Things vv. 18-19

> 8:18–19 The word of the LORD who rules over all came to me as follows: "The LORD who rules over all says, 'The fast of the fourth, fifth, seventh, and tenth months will become joyful and happy, pleasant feasts for the house of Judah, so love truth and peace.'

The prophet now returns to the original question of fasting (7:3). Having explained the purposes of God relevant to their return from exile, involving the forgiveness of the nation's sin and their restoration to both spiritual and material prosperity, Zechariah concludes that the fasts commemorating the destruction of the temple and the events which accompanied it (see notes on 7:3) should be changed into a celebration of the return and restoration. The former things were to be forgotten, and God would wipe away all the tears of those days from their eyes.

A Future Ingathering of All Nations vv. 20-32

> *8:20–23 The LORD who rules over all says, 'It will someday come to pass that people — residents of many cities — will come. The inhabitants of one will go to another and say, "Let's go up at once to ask the favor of the LORD, to seek the LORD who rules over all. Indeed, I'll go with you." 'Many peoples and powerful nations will come to Jerusalem to seek the LORD who rules over all and to ask his favor. The LORD who rules over all says, 'In those days ten people from all languages and nations will grasp hold of — indeed, grab — the robe of one Jew and say, "Let us go with you, for we have heard that God is with you." ' "*

God looks ahead and gives Zechariah a glimpse of his greater purposes for Israel. He had restored Israel because of his love for her—but also that through her he might show his love to all nations. Israel was never allowed to lose sight of this overarching purpose of God throughout the ministry of the prophets—so it is strange that they did so by the time of the early church! God details how it was his will for many Gentiles from all nations (apparently more in number than the believing Jews) would eagerly come and seek the Lord and be joined to faithful Jews in their worship of God. This promise was not entirely fulfilled until Jesus came and the church began; for then as the word of the Lord went out from Jerusalem, many were brought to God, who would from that time on be worshipped not in Jerusalem only, but by people everywhere in Spirit and truth (John 4:24).

Discussion Questions for Chapter 8

1. vv.1–8. Think of a difficult situation in your life, or in the life of your church. It may be that nothing can be done about these problems—but is anything too hard for the Lord? Reflect on this.

2. vv.8–15. God's Spirit motivated the people to cooperate in his sovereign purpose. In what ways might you also be part of God's work in the coming week?

3. vv16–32. List several responsibilities that Christians have as a result of God's mercy toward them.

Chapter 9

Introduction to Chapters 9–14

Many scholars consider that chapters 9–14 represent an entirely separate literary unit from chapters 1–8 and attribute these two to differing authors. However, for the purposes of this study, we shall assume that if any non-Zechariah material is present that it is because Zechariah is employing material from other earlier prophets to illustrate his message to the nation. As for setting the context for these messages, it appears to me that he messages of chapters 8–14 contain a good deal of content which might have been relevant to the returning exiles.[12]

Prophecies Against Israel's Enemies

> *9:1 This is a message from the LORD: His eyes are on everyone, especially the tribes of Israel. So he pronounces judgment against the cities of Hadrach and Damascus. (CEV)*

An oracle is a heavy burden, a prophetic message which weighed the prophet down because of its gravity and seriousness. The oracle concerns the nations along the Mediterranean coast which were Israel's enemies and neighbours—Syria and Philistia. Originally, when Israel invaded the Promised Land, God included these territories in their inheritance (Num. 34:5–6); but Israel had never conquered them completely.

---

[12] For a defence of the unity of the Book of Zechariah see James A. Hartle, "The Literary Unity of Zechariah", *JETS* 35/2 (June 1992), pp. 145–157

Hadrach was to the north of Hamath, and Hamath was nearer to the Syrian capital Damascus. Tyre and Sidon were also along this same coast.

The prophet speaks of the defeat of these fortresses as coming from the Lord, without naming the armies responsible or giving further details of the time and circumstances of these conquests. For this reason experts argue over the dates of these prophecies (and consequently whether or not they were all written by Zechariah). It is possible that each verse depicts a different time in history. Baldwin explains that some suppose the defeat of Hamath and Damascus by Jeroboam II to be depicted here (2 Kgs. 14:28); but it is also true that the Assyrians and Greeks fought these cities in later times, and that it was Alexander the Great who eventually overcame Tyre. The Philistine cities mentioned in verses 5 and 6 were subdued by Nebuchadrezzar before the exile, and so some scholars suppose that this is an earlier prophecy inserted by the editor.[13]

The key to why this allusion of God's actions against Israel's enemies is made by the prophet is found in verse 8. Many of the returned exiles faced hostility from the surrounding nations (e.g. Neh. 2:10), and God wanted to reassure them that he would keep them safe from enemy invasion. Clearly this promise was not open ended—Jerusalem and the temple were much later invaded by the Romans—but it was a promise which held for that time. God's eyes were upon the children of Israel to watch over and guard them, just as his eyes were upon their enemies in order to bring calamity on them. I have quoted the CEV above because I think it is a better rendering than those translations which suggest humanity's eyes being on the Lord.

---

[13] Baldwin, pp. 157–158

> *9:2–4 as are those of Hamath also, which adjoins Damascus, and Tyre and Sidon, though they consider themselves to be very wise. Tyre built herself a fortification and piled up silver like dust and gold like the mud of the streets! Nevertheless the Lord will evict her and shove her fortifications into the sea — she will be consumed by fire.*

Using its wisdom—the technology available in those days—the island of Tyre had built an almost impenetrable sea defence, and became a wealthy trade centre. Nevertheless, Alexander overcame these defences 'by building a mole from the mainland'[14] and dealt ruthlessly with the people of Tyre. It never again rose to power.

> *9:5-7 Ashkelon will see and be afraid; Gaza will be in great anguish, as will Ekron, for her hope will have been dried up. Gaza will lose her king, and Ashkelon will no longer be inhabited. A mongrel people will live in Ashdod, for I will greatly humiliate the Philistines. I will take away their abominable religious practices; then those who survive will become a community of believers in our God, like a clan in Judah, and Ekron will be like the Jebusites.*

What is interesting about the depicted humbling of the Philistines is that God would use it to bring them into fellowship with himself and his people. They were to be absorbed into the population of Israel just as the Jebusites (the original inhabitants of Jerusalem) had been by David when he took Jerusalem. It was necessary of course for their religious practices to change for this to become possible.

---

[14] Baldwin, p. 160

Nevertheless, perhaps it was not until the days of the early church that this scripture was entirely fulfilled. For when Philip came to this region (Acts 8:40), it seems many were added to the Lord, and the text of Acts shows how they were commanded to abstain from blood and food sacrificed to idols, and from sexual immorality. With these 'abominable practices' removed by the grace of Christ, they became fully accepted as part of the renewed people of God; that is, Jews and Gentiles were made equal partners in God's new believing community (Eph. 2:15).

The Lord Defends His People

> *9:8 Then I will surround my temple to protect it like a guard from anyone crossing back and forth; so no one will cross over against them anymore as an oppressor, for now I myself have seen it.*

Whilst this verse refers in the first instance to the temple itself, its message encompasses the whole nation which was home to that temple. God would be on guard and keep watch ('*I myself have seen it*') over his people continually. Baldwin[15] notes the structure of this poem follows that of the earlier verses, and so we might infer the unity of this chapter's composition, even if it was a redaction of various original sources. Nevertheless, the details of this section remain somewhat obscure and it requires a good deal of interpretation of the context in order to understand them. We will assume the messages to be relevant to the post exilic period; although they also contain a good deal of Messianic allusions.[16] Whatever the

---

[15] Baldwin, p. 163
[16] David Baron, *Zechariah: A Commentary on His Visions & Prophecies* (Grand Rapids: Kregel, 1918), p. 6

circumstances and time of the prophecy, the truth expounded to God's people is enduring. God would uphold and defend the cause of his own people and fulfil his purpose for the nations in relation to the coming of the Messiah King.

The Coming King and His Reign of Abundance and Peace

> *9:9 Rejoice greatly, daughter of Zion! Shout, daughter of Jerusalem! Look! Your king is coming to you: he is legitimate and victorious, humble and riding on a donkey — on a young donkey, the foal of a female donkey.*

This verse was used by the gospel writers to relate to the time of Christ's entry into Jerusalem (Matt. 21:5; John 12:15). The rightful and eternal King of Israel comes with meekness, riding the young unbroken colt, accompanied by its mother, into the city of Jerusalem to shouts of rejoicing and cries of 'hosanna'. As Zechariah depicts, he comes bringing salvation; though the nature of that salvation was until his death and resurrection quite unknown to humanity.

> *9:10 I will remove the chariot from Ephraim and the warhorse from Jerusalem, and the battle bow will be removed. Then he will announce peace to the nations. His dominion will be from sea to sea and from the Euphrates River to the ends of the earth.*

The Messiah being King over Israel is not the total extent of his glory. He will reign from sea to sea, from the River Euphrates to the ends of the earth. This is a worldwide reign of peace—and the verse insists that it is only the Christ who will introduce this peace to the nations.

The chariot, war horse and bow were the artillery, cavalry and infantry of the ancient world. Today one might think in terms of the removal of tanks, war planes and guns, but the picture is the same. The reign of Christ over the earth will bring an end to war.

> *9:11–12 Moreover, as for you, because of our covenant relationship secured with blood, I will release your prisoners from the waterless pit. Return to the stronghold, you prisoners, with hope; today I declare that I will return double what was taken from you.*

There is some debate over who the prisoners are who are in this waterless pit, and what that pit represents. It may be that God is promising the removal of affliction and famine conditions, to restore his exiled people to the stronghold of Jerusalem and to bless them with a measure that would outweigh the pain of their exile in captivity.

On the other hand, the verse can be used to describe the work which Christ has achieved through his introduction of a new covenant ratified by his own blood shed on the cross. He has delivered those who were prisoners of sin and Satan and who therefore were without the living water of a relationship with God and who were doomed to an eternity in the waterless pit of hell where 'the fire is not quenched' (Mark 9:43). In this case, the stronghold referred to would be God our refuge, or even Christ our refuge (Heb. 6:18) who rescues us from the wrath to come (1 Thess. 1:10). As for the 'double' (i.e. abundant) restoration of God's blessings upon those redeemed by Christ's blood, these could be enumerated at length from many New Testament writers. As Isaac Watts in his hymn 'Jesus Shall Reign' succinctly notes, 'In him the tribes of Adam boast more blessings than their father lost.'

> *9:13–14 I will bend Judah as my bow; I will load the bow with Ephraim, my arrow! I will stir up your sons, Zion, against yours, Greece, and I will make you, Zion, like a warrior's sword. Then the LORD will appear above them, and his arrow will shoot forth like lightning; the Lord GOD will blow the trumpet and will sally forth on the southern storm winds.*

We may be uncertain of the exact circumstances in which this promise was given. Perhaps the returned exiles feared the rising power of Greece, or perhaps this note was inserted by a later writer to encourage Israel at a time when the Greeks actually did invade the land. Actually, the mention of Greece has been omitted by some translators altogether, who see in this verse a broader reference to God's victory over all nations. Whatever the case, the overarching message of the text remains clear. God is not helpless against his enemies. He is able to take hold of human weakness and glorify his name. Nor will he abandon his chosen people, for he will take hold of little Judah and Ephraim to defeat far more powerful foes; he will take hold of the foolish to confound the wise and the weak to confound the strong (1 Cor. 1:27–29). In the picture given in verse 14 we see God acting on behalf of his people, regardless of human agency.

We might be weak, foolish and few, but the Lord can give victory to his people by his own supernatural agency.

> *9:15 The LORD who rules over all will guard them, and they will prevail and overcome with sling stones. Then they will drink, and will become noisy like drunkards, full like the sacrificial basin or like the corners of the altar.*

No matter what weapons come against the people of God (here sling stones may be used against them as much as by them) they will overcome because it is God who guards them. Their victory will be complete; as symbolised by the fullness of their cups, (not actually cups of alcoholic drink nor blood, but full cups of blessing brought about by the blood of the new covenant)—a fullness further symbolised by the basins used in the temple to collect the blood of sacrifices (Lev. 4:7). The noise of the victorious crowd, although resembling that of drunkards, owes its origin to a more noble cause; as was seen on the Day of Pentecost as the fullness of the Spirit becomes the church's possession as a spoil of Christ's absolute victory (Acts 2:15; Eph. 5:18).

> *9:16 On that day the LORD their God will deliver them as the flock of his people, for they are the precious stones of a crown sparkling over his land.*

God's people with whom he has made his covenant are precious to him: they are the flock of which he is pleased to be the shepherd, and they are the crown of his glory – as the writer of Ephesians explains, nothing will so glorify God throughout eternity as those whom he has redeemed by his grace (Eph. 1:12).

> *9:17 For how great is his goodness, and how great is his beauty! corn shall make the young men cheerful, and new wine the maids. (AV)*

I have elected to use the Authorised Version for this verse, since it seems to make better sense. Admittedly, the subject (who is great in goodness and beauty?) is unclear in this verse, but perhaps in context it is in praise of all that God has done. God's grace itself is a beautiful treasure; and the objects of grace are also made beautiful by him (Eph. 5:25–27). His abundant blessing (symbolised by new wine and grain) is poured out on all, whether male or female.

Baldwin sees in this a more direct reference to God not only protecting his people but also providing for them. There was to be no more famine, but sufficient rain to produce bumper crops, if God's people would entreat him for it (10:1); and this would result in great rejoicing throughout this pastoral society of Judah. Nevertheless, Baldwin points further to the abiding spiritual significance of these words. To be alienated from God is to be in an arid and barren place; whereas to be reconciled to God is to be blessed in unspeakably bountiful terms.[17]

Discussion Questions for Chapter 9

1. vv.1–7. Why do you think God speaks to his people about his judgments upon their enemies?

2. List the ways in which God says he will provide deliverance, salvation and protection for his people.

3. In what ways do you think that verse 9 might offer a prophetic description of Jesus?

---

[17] Baldwin, p. 170

Chapter 10

The Abundant Blessing of the Lord
10:1 Ask the LORD for rain in the season of the late spring rains — the LORD who causes thunderstorms — and he will give everyone showers of rain and green growth in the field.

At the end of chapter 9 we saw the blessing of God on an arable farming community described in terms of overflowing harvests of grain and new wine. The picture of abundance continues with an exhortation to pray during times of blessing and restoration; for when God is looking favourably on his land and his people he will be inquired of to pour out even more abundant blessing (in this case the late spring rains which would help to produce higher crop yields). Even though we may not live in farming community, the spiritual principle abides; we cannot simply hope for the outpouring of God's blessing—we must ask in order to receive (Matt. 7:7).

God as the Good Shepherd
10:2 For the household gods have spoken wickedness, the soothsayers have seen a lie, and as for the dreamers, they have disclosed emptiness and give comfort in vain. Therefore the people set out like sheep and become scattered because they have no shepherd.

The idolatry of the nation had led them into spiritual poverty and moral wickedness, resulting in their exile. The worship of idols had brought no benefit to the nation; it offered them neither comfort nor hope for the future. In this way Israel had become like sheep without a shepherd, with no one to provide for, bless or shelter them.

10:3 Mine anger was kindled against the shepherds, and I punished the goats: for the LORD of hosts hath visited his flock the house of Judah, and hath made them as his goodly horse in the battle. (AV)

The time had come for God to show Israel the contrast between the blessings to be found in the true worship of Jehovah and the worthless worship of idols. God would gather the people of Judah like a shepherd gathers his flock, to protect, bless and provide for them. Although their idols had done them no good, God would bless them and do them a great deal of good, and only good. The AV (above) seems to me more correctly to employ the past tense, showing how God *had been* angered and *had punished* those who had led Israel astray with their lying teachings. This allusion to punishment is probably a reference to the Babylonian invasion and the years of exile; for it appears that by the time of the return, the priests were ready to obey God's will (Neh. 10:28).

As their shepherd, God would take good care of them; just as a man might feed, groom and in other ways look after the horse he rides; and upon which, in time of war, his life might depend.

Jesus took up the imagery of God being the good shepherd and used it to denote his own relationship with his people in John 10:1–30. Again, Jesus used this image to stress the difference between false religious teachers and himself; he emphasised how these 'thieves' only came to kill and destroy, whereas he had come 'that you might have life to the full' (John 10:10). Those who were part of Jesus' flock were superbly blessed, and assured of everlasting security – 'none shall pluck them out of my hand' (John 10:28).

10:4 From him will come the cornerstone, the wall peg, the battle bow, and every ruler.

This prophecy initially seems superfluous; for Israel already knew that its kings were to come only from Judah and no other tribe (Gen. 49:10). Yet it may have served as an encouragement for the exiles to know that their governor was from this tribe, and that God upheld and recognised him as their true leader and head of state. The ruler of the nation held the people together, as the cornerstone supports the wall, or the nail firmly fixes an item in place. It was he who led the people into battle and gave judgment on all important matters of state, being supreme over his counsellors and generals.

Yet one cannot help tasting the Messianic flavour of this prophecy. For God would one day reveal the good shepherd as one who came from Judah to rule over all people. This shepherd, Jesus Christ, would become the chief cornerstone, on which the whole church would be built. He would be the nail fixed in a firm place on which a person might believe and not be ashamed; as one might trust a firm nail not to give way under the weight of a coat placed on it (Rom. 9:33). And how firm he is! Since he lives in the power of an endless life he is able to save to the uttermost all that come to God through him (Heb. 7:25). With regard to battle, Christ is depicted in the Book of Revelation as riding a war horse with a sharp two edged sword; the picture is of Christ as the conqueror who is victorious over all (Rev. 19:11); as the supreme ruler, none can deny Christ, for he is the King of Kings and Lord of Lords (Rev. 19:16).

Rejoicing in God's Victory

10:5 And they will be like warriors trampling the mud of the streets in battle. They will fight, for the LORD will be with them, and will defeat the enemy cavalry.

Note that the prophet announces 'they will be *like* warriors'; he does not predict here any particular battle, but rather illustrates the invincibility of God's people when they come under his protection and care. The picture is one of victory, and corresponds well with Paul's idea of the victory which God's people possess since God is on their side (Rom. 8:31).

Nevertheless, in the second sentence, a battle is predicted, in which Israel wins against all odds, for God is with them. One does not need to conjecture which enemy was defeated—the lesson the prophet wishes to communicate is that those who have God on their side are always victorious. One person, standing with God, is in a majority.

10:6 "I (says the LORD) will strengthen the kingdom of Judah and deliver the people of Joseph and will bring them back because of my compassion for them. They will be as though I had never rejected them, for I am the LORD their God and therefore I will hear them.

God announced his purpose in order to establish it in the minds of the returned exiles, and perhaps to motivate those still in faraway lands to return. God would have compassion on the nation of Israel; restoring them and forgiving their past transgressions as if these and the exile had never happened. Since God was their God by an everlasting covenant he would not turn a deaf ear to them. The greatest privilege any nation can have is an open invitation to appeal to the listening ear of God.

The theme is again taken up by the writers of the New Testament in terms of forgiveness being the gift of God's compassionate love (Eph. 2:4), and of its being complete (Heb. 10:2). Zechariah, of course, refers to the sin of the nation corporately, whereas modern readers of the New Testament tend to apply the promise to each individual believer (though in reality it is still the church *as a whole* which is pictured as experiencing the forgiveness and receiving the promise). The writer to the Hebrews alludes to God 'remembering their sins no more' (Jer. 31:34; Heb. 8:12) and clearly, when sin is forgiven in this way, the open heaven promised by Zechariah becomes available to those who are forgiven. The New Testament is filled with exhortations to pray and believe that God hears the prayers of believers (Mark 11:24); yet the superficial and half-hearted way in which some believers approach prayer reveals them to have a limited faith and a diminished awareness of the character of God.

10:7 The Ephraimites will be like warriors and will rejoice as if they had drunk wine. Their children will see it and rejoice; they will celebrate in the things of the LORD.

The rejoicing of warriors celebrating a great victory may again be pictorial rather than the prophetic prediction of a battle; for the children are portrayed as joining in the rejoicing and the source of their joy is not defeat of their enemies, but the Lord. Of all the gifts of God, it is his spiritual blessings rather than his temporal deliverances which are most to be valued; and these were known even among the people of the Old Covenant. Yet they are to be experienced to a far greater measure by those who have entered into the New Covenant (Eph. 1:3).

10:8–10 I will signal for them and gather them, for I have already redeemed them; then they will become as numerous as they were before. Though I scatter them among the nations, they will remember in far-off places — they and their children will sprout forth and return. I will bring them back from Egypt and gather them from Assyria. I will bring them to the lands of Gilead and Lebanon, for there will not be enough room for them in their own land.

God had previously brought his people out of Egypt and made them his peculiar possession (Exod. 19:5). It is his abiding covenant love which lay behind his restoring them to the land and increasing their numbers to repopulate it. Wherever they had settled since the exile, God would call them to return, and so many would heed the call that they would have to settle in nearby Lebanon and Gilead due to the land being too densely populated.

10:11–12 The LORD will cross the sea of storms and will calm its turbulence. The depths of the Nile will dry up, the pride of Assyria will be humbled, and the domination of Egypt will be no more. Thus I will strengthen them by my power, and they will walk about in my name," says the LORD.

The details of this prophecy may be obscure to us today, but its root meaning is clear. Whatever problems affect the people of God, God promises to act on their behalf; whether it is to still the angry waves of trouble which oppress them or to subdue the proud nations which threaten them. God's people are invincible so long as he is among them; so they will walk in his strength, overcoming all obstacles, not by might or power, but by the Spirit of God.

Discussion Questions for Chapter 10

1. vv.1–4. In what ways might the allusions in these verses be applied to Jesus (the good shepherd, a nail in a firm place, etc.)?

2. vv. 5–7. In these verses, on what does God base his promise to hear the prayers of his people?

3. vv. 7–12. How might God's dealings with Israel in these verses fill the believer with confidence today?

Chapter 11

The Mighty will be Humbled

> *11:1–3 Open your gates, Lebanon, so that the fire may consume your cedars. Howl, fir tree, because the cedar has fallen; the majestic trees have been destroyed. Howl, oaks of Bashan, because the impenetrable forest has fallen. Listen to the howling of shepherds, because their magnificence has been destroyed. Listen to the roaring of young lions, because the thickets of the Jordan have been devastated.*

At first reading this passage appears to deal with God's judgement of the nation of Lebanon, but this is not altogether certain. Many earlier commentators regarded the allusion to Lebanon and cedars as a reference to the temple in Jerusalem which had been lined with cedar from Lebanon. This temple had been burned by the king of Babylon many years before the exile, and so an insertion of a prophecy at this point by Zechariah would suggest that he was rehearsing history in order to make a point.[18] An alternative view is that the destruction of Herod's temple by Titus is prophesied here, but this seems less likely.

Cedars and tall trees in the scripture represent human pride and sinful independence of God, and were often used to depict proud and cruel leaders (e.g. Isa. 2:13). Similarly, images of shepherds and lions are used to designate rulers (e.g. Jer. 25:34–37; Jer. 50:44). God will

---

[18] Remember that throughout these studies I am proposing that Zechariah really was the author of this book at the time of the return of the exiles and the rebuilding of the second temple.

always humble the proud; as he did through the sacking of Jerusalem by the Babylonians and as he would do again through its destruction at the hands of the Romans. Could this be another warning from Israel's history, as God foresees the nation, albeit now returned from exile and for a time eagerly serving him, reverting to the old ways of pride, idolatry and corruption?

The Rejection of the Good Shepherd

> *11:4 The LORD my God says this: "Shepherd the flock set aside for slaughter.*

This section clearly refers to the nation of Israel and its spiritual leaders (shepherds). Zechariah has been appointed by God as a shepherd over Israel in order to tend and feed them (Matthew Henry refers to him as a type of Christ in this regard). Unfortunately, as he is permitted to know from the start, they will not respond to his shepherding, and as a result God has already decided, figuratively in this instance, to set them apart for slaughter, meaning they would be rejected by him.

> *11:5 Those who buy them slaughter them and are not held guilty; those who sell them say, 'Blessed be the LORD, for I am rich.' Their own shepherds have no compassion for them.*

This verse implies that corruption had again become rife among the people of God, with bribery in law courts and possibly the reduction of poor debtors and their families to slaves being alluded to here. Moreover, it was the spiritual leaders of the nation who profited from this corruption; and so brazen were they in their evil doing that they dared to bless God for the money they had made dishonestly.

> *11:6 Indeed, I will no longer have compassion on the people of the land," says the LORD, "but instead I will turn every last person over to his neighbor and his king. They will devastate the land, and I will not deliver it from them."*

Where such implacability dominated the land, God had to make clear that he would show no mercy to those who showed no mercy to others. This puts Jesus' words, 'Blessed are the merciful for they shall obtain mercy', into their historical context. Jesus was challenging the corruption and extortion of his times, and insisting, as does James, that 'mercy triumphs over judgment' (Jms. 2:13).

> *11:7 So I began to shepherd the flock destined for slaughter, the most afflicted of all the flock. Then I took two staffs, calling one "Pleasantness" and the other "Binders," and I tended the flock.*

Yet it was not to the corrupt leaders but to the poor and oppressed people of Israel to whom the shepherd was sent—even as Christ came to proclaim good news to the poor, to heal the sick and give sight to the blind. Zechariah, again depicting Christ, fed the people God's word as a good shepherd on the basis of grace and loving-kindness ('pleasantness' and 'binders' stand for that by which God binds and unites us to himself in Christ, namely his love).

> *11:8 Next I eradicated the three shepherds in one month, for I ran out of patience with them and, indeed, they detested me as well.*

The good shepherd is here seen deposing three other shepherds in a verse about which scholars simply cannot agree—in fact many admit they can never identify these three shepherds. What is clear is that God's face is set against the religious leaders who devour his flock.

It is also apparent that although the good shepherd did so much to tend and feed the sheep on the basis of grace and love, yet they became obstinate and hardened, rejecting the rule of their shepherd in favour of the oppression of their leaders! In a similar way, the Jews of Jesus' time rejected God's will and purpose (Luke 7:30) and Jesus as the promised Messiah (Mark 12:20; Luke 17:25).

> *11:9 I then said, "I will not shepherd you. What is to die, let it die, and what is to be eradicated, let it be eradicated. As for those who survive, let them eat each other's flesh!"*

Because they rejected him, the shepherd in turn rejects the flock and leaves them to fend for themselves. This is the gravest principle of God's dealings with humankind. Those who harden, resist and rebel are given over to their own stubborn hearts and become reprobates, unable to be redeemed for they have silenced the pleading and loving voice of God. To reject the good shepherd is to invite disaster, a picture which Jesus also built upon (John 3:36).

> *11:10 Then I took my staff "Pleasantness" and cut it in two to annul my covenant that I had made with all the people.*

The image here is not of God's one-sided annulling of his covenant. The picture is somewhat more complex. The good shepherd had announced to them God's message of love and grace, but they put themselves outside of his covenant by rejecting that message.

Until Christ, the Jews were in covenant with God, but Christ established the new covenant to replace the old, which was meant to be a shadow of the new. It was not that God had rejected Israel, but that he had always intended for them to embrace the new covenant as a continuation, or fulfilment and completion of the old. Yet some did not accept Christ, the good shepherd, and the way of salvation which he had made for them on the cross, and so the prophet announces that not only were they not in convent relation to God in the new covenant sense. Indeed, by rejecting Christ they had negated their involvement in the old covenant as well. The Jews who believed continued to be part of God's people, although now in an even fuller sense; yet the Jews who rejected Christ no longer had any relationship to God at all. He would no longer be their shepherd. They were cut off from among their people (Acts 3:23).

Note that Paul emphasises the possibility of their being restored to covenant if they did not persist in unbelief but turned in faith to Christ (Rom. 11:23).

> *11:11 So it was annulled that very day, and then the most afflicted of the flock who kept faith with me knew that that was the word of the LORD.*

There were those, a small flock, who are described as the poorest and most afflicted among the people (1 Cor. 1:27–29) who remained faithful to the good shepherd even as a small group remained loyal to Jesus of Galilee (Acts 1:13–14).

It is interesting to note how this theme relates to that of the opening verses 11:1–3, in as much as the proclamation that Christ's death is the means of inclusion in God's new covenant people quells all human pride and appeals to the poor and weak.

> 11:12–13 Then I said to them, "If it seems good to you, pay me my wages, but if not, forget it." So they weighed out my payment — thirty pieces of silver. The LORD then said to me, "Throw to the potter that exorbitant sum at which they valued me!" So I took the thirty pieces of silver and threw them to the potter at the temple of the LORD.

Here is the famous prophecy used by Matthew to describe the betrayal of Judas Iscariot. By doing so Matthew is tapping into the imagery of the good shepherd. For the background of Jesus' betrayal by Judas was Jesus' rejection by Israel; and the price of his betrayal was thirty pieces of silver. Although this was the price of a slave, it was still a large amount of money. God's law ensured that human life carried a high price (Exod. 21:32). Matthew explains the fulfilment of the latter part of this verse in terms of Judas returning the money to the temple, and the chief priests using it to by the potter's field as a burial ground for foreigners. This indicates the level of contempt in which the religious leaders held their good shepherd. They valued Christ as much as they valued contaminated burial ground for despised Gentiles.

> 11:14 Then I cut the second staff "Binders" in two in order to annul the covenant of brotherhood between Judah and Israel.

Disunity within Israel would be the result of the rejection of the good shepherd. Jesus expands on this theme, including not only the break up between those Jews who believed in him and those who did not, but also that which would occur in families, where some would be Christ's and others not (Matt. 10:35-36). It was just such a division which led to the separation of the Christian church from Judaism in the first century.

> *11:15 Again the LORD said to me, "Take up once more the equipment of a foolish shepherd.*

Those who would not heed the good shepherd would be the prey of the foolish shepherds. Everyone needs a spiritual leader. If we will not come to Christ we will remain in Satan's power (Eph. 2:2). False religion is recognised by its lack of grace and love. The false shepherds care only for themselves and not the flock, as Jesus warned 'the thief comes not but to steal and to kill and destroy' (John 10:10).

> *11:16 Indeed, I am about to raise up a shepherd in the land who will not take heed to the sheep headed to slaughter, will not seek the scattered, and will not heal the injured. Moreover, he will not nourish the one that is healthy but instead will eat the meat of the fat sheep and tear off their hooves.*

Verse 16 serves in a way as a promise, for what the foolish shepherd does not do is by inference what the good shepherd *will* do for his people—caring, gathering, healing and feeding them.

> *11:17 Woe to the worthless shepherd who abandons the flock! May a sword fall on his arm and his right eye! May his arm wither completely away, and his right eye become completely blind!"*

Those who deceive and lead humankind away from the truth were called 'blind guides' by Christ who insisted that they and their followers would both 'fall into the pit' (Matt. 15:14). These verses imply that Zechariah may also have encountered false teachers who tried to lead Israel away from God. The false teachers will share in God's punishment because of their opposition to Christ who longs to gather the people like sheep who are lost without a shepherd.

Discussion Questions for Chapter 11

1. vv.1–6. In what way does the good shepherd differ from the other shepherds mentioned here?

2. In what way did failure to accept the good shepherd lead to division within Israel?

3. What do you think is being represented by the 'foolish shepherd' of vv. 15–17.

Chapter 12

God's End-Time Dealings with all Nations

> *12:1 The revelation of the word of the LORD concerning Israel: The LORD — he who stretches out the heavens and lays the foundations of the earth, who forms the human spirit within a person — says,*

It is always essential to pay attention to a God given revelation, for once God makes his word known it will surely come to pass; and this particular revelation concerned his dealings with the nation of Israel and its relationship with the nations. God introduces himself as the creator of the vast universe who has given to every human being a living soul, inferring that we are all therefore accountable to him.

> *12:2 "I am about to make Jerusalem a cup that brings dizziness to all the surrounding nations; indeed, Judah will also be included when Jerusalem is besieged.*

God's purpose to bring judgment against all nations would centre upon Jerusalem and seems to involve God's gathering of all nations to the area of Judah around Jerusalem to make war. Such an event has never historically happened, but in the book of Revelation a day is predicted when God will gather the standing armies of all nations to the plains of Megiddo in the valley of Armageddon (Rev. 16:16). They will show their final rejection of God's rule by uniting there to fight against the returning Lord Jesus Christ as he descends to earth. It is quite possible that the visions in Revelation and Zechariah may offer different perspectives of the same period in time. The enmity of the human heart against God is here fully manifested, for whether they are attacking the place where his name dwells (Jerusalem and the temple) or attacking his son, the people's rebellion against God's reign is inflexible and so will lead to their final judgment; for God's victory is assured (Ps. 2:1–5).

> *12:3 Moreover, on that day I will make Jerusalem a heavy burden for all the nations, and all who try to carry it will be seriously injured; yet all the peoples of the earth will be assembled against it.*

When all the nations gather against Jerusalem to destroy it, they shall be unable to do so. God says he will make Jerusalem like a heavy stone. If you have ever tried to move a huge boulder single-handed, you will appreciate the picture here: it will be just as futile for the nations to attempt to remove Jerusalem. I once remember moving a wooden shed from one side of my mother's garden to the other. It took four men, and we stumbled and fell several times risking injury. In this way those who attack Jerusalem will only succeed in harming themselves. This may actually be true throughout the time of the end as well as during the final battle predicted in Revelation.

> *12:4 In that day," says the LORD, "I will strike every horse with confusion and its rider with madness. I will pay close attention to the house of Judah, but will strike all the horses of the nations with blindness.*

The picture of blinded horses indicates that the attempts of the nations to frustrate God's purposes will be futile. Can you imagine the effectiveness of a horseman charging in to battle on a blind horse? Yet despite the futility of the attempt, God has hardened the hearts of his wicked opponents so that they will persist in fighting against him until they are all destroyed. They have refused the love of the truth and so God will bring on them a strong delusion that will believe the lie—believing that humanity might conquer its creator (2 Thess. 2:11–12)!

> *12:5 Then the leaders of Judah will say to themselves, 'The inhabitants of Jerusalem are a means of strength to us through their God, the LORD who rules over all.'*

All those who dwell in Jerusalem at that time shall, together with their leaders, realise and acknowledge that the almighty God is their strength and protection (Ps. 46:1), and that he reigns over all (Isa. 52:7).

> *12:6 On that day I will make the leaders of Judah like an igniter among sticks and a burning torch among sheaves, and they will burn up all the surrounding nations right and left. Then the people of Jerusalem will settle once more in their place, the city of Jerusalem.*

The means of God's enemies' destruction is here depicted as being the leaders of Judah, the royal tribe. The true leader of Judah will likewise come at the end of time to punish God's enemies with eternal fire (Rev. 19:19–20), and settle Jerusalem again with his faithful people.

> *12:7 The LORD also will deliver the homes of Judah first, so that the splendour of the kingship of David and of the people of Jerusalem may not exceed that of Judah.*

In this picture, Judah will share in the victory with her king. In God's victory, special place will be given to the royal tribe; and no wonder, for Jesus Christ himself comes from this tribe, and will be their glory. He will be our glory too, for we will gladly see him reign over all the earth. Yet it is God's purpose that Christ (forever exalted yet forever meek of heart) will share his glory with us—and we too shall reign with him upon earth (2 Tim. 2:12; Rev. 5:10; Matt. 5:5).

> *12:8 On that day the LORD himself will defend the inhabitants of Jerusalem, so that the weakest among them will be like mighty David, and the dynasty of David will be like God, like the angel of the LORD before them.*

Not only at the time of the end, but at all times, God's people are invincible. The fire could not overcome them, nor lions, and nor will the armies of the nation overwhelm them. If God be for us, who can be against us? The weakest saint will be terrible like a mighty warrior in that day; for they will accompany the King of kings riding white horses behind him in his victory train (Rev. 19:14).

> *12:9 So on that day I will set out to destroy all the nations that come against Jerusalem."*

The result of God's overwhelming victory against his enemies will be their destruction in battle (Rev. 19:21) and their everlasting punishment (Rev. 20:15).

God's End-Time Dealings with Israel

> *12:10–14 "I will pour out on the kingship of David and the population of Jerusalem a spirit of grace and supplication so that they will look to me, the one they have pierced. They will lament for him as one laments for an only son, and there will be a bitter cry for him like the bitter cry for a firstborn. On that day the lamentation in Jerusalem will be as great as the lamentation at Hadad-Rimmon in the plain of Megiddo. The land will mourn, clan by clan — the*

> *clan of the royal household of David by itself and their wives by themselves; the clan of the family of Nathan by itself and their wives by themselves; the clan of the descendants of Levi by itself and their wives by themselves; and the clan of the Shimeites by itself and their wives by themselves — all the clans that remain, each separately with their wives."*

If at the time of the end, God will deal with the God-rejecting nations in wrath and judgment, yet he has a different purpose for dealing with Israel. Clearly it will be during a time of danger and distress—why else would all the families be split up, with wives and children separated from their husbands?[19] Yet during this time of sorrow, God will pour out a spirit of 'grace and supplication' connected with the death in the city—at the hands of the people of Israel—of a certain person whom God clearly recognises as being closely connected with himself. In fact, God says that it was 'me' whom they pierced.

The crucifixion of Christ was followed by the destruction of Jerusalem, an event which does not fit well with this prophecy if it is to be understood in terms both of the nation lamenting over God's righteous servant and also in view of the invincibility of Jerusalem (v. 3). That is why I consider that an eschatological re-application of this prophecy is appropriate. Either just before Christ's return , or at the very point of his return, Israel will mourn over the wasted years she spent without God by rejecting his only son Jesus Christ who was pierced for her iniquities in order to provide a fountain for cleansing

---

[19] Merrill notes that the clan of Nathan was by now acknowledged as the royal line. Eugene H. Merrill , *Haggai, Zechariah, Malachi: An Exegetical Commentary* (Richardson: Biblical Studies Press, 2013), p. 285

from sin. At this time there will be a national acknowledgment of this error combined with national repentance; each survivor of Israel giving his or her own allegiance to Christ. And so, in the midst of suffering and dreadful circumstances, in an apocalyptic vision concerning the end of time, Zechariah sees what Paul later saw, that God's ultimate purpose would be the restoration of Israel, just as she had longed and hoped for (Rom. 11:26).

Discussion Questions for Chapter 12

1. Why are all nations accountable to God?

2. In what way would God use Israel to punish the nations, and why?

3. We have discussed how Zechariah's prophecy may have been re-applied by the New Testament writers to speak of a future day in which the nation that had crucified the Messiah would repent and turn to God. How does Zechariah's prophecy describe this repentance?

Chapter 13

The Shepherd of My People:
The Wounding of God's Shepherd Provides Cleansing from Sin

Sin Forgiven

> *13:1 "In that day there will be a fountain opened up for the dynasty of David and the people of Jerusalem to cleanse them from sin and impurity.*

God through the prophet chooses his words deliberately. Unlike a lake, where the water might stagnate, a fountain is an ever flowing stream of fresh water. And a naturally occurring spring is set here in contrast to a well—for wells are dug by man's effort whilst springs or fountains bubble up from the earth because of the action of the Creator. In this way the verse reveals that God himself would deal with human sin, providing a way for cleansing. This opening would be made by God's action upon earth, just as a spring bubbles up from the ground.

The Jews knew and understood the image of water cleansing away their sin (Ps. 119:9, 11); it was through obedience to the Torah that men could avoid sinful paths (Ps. 19:7–11). Yet God had spoken to them through the prophets that as he sprinkled clean water on them to make them clean, he would write his law within their hearts (Jer. 31:33–34; Ezek. 36:25–27). This would lead to obedience, not to the letter of the law, but to its spirit. Jesus similarly recognised the cleansing power of God's word when he said 'You are clean already because of the word that I have spoken to you' (John 15:3 see also Eph. 5:25–26).

Yet the Jews also knew and understood that according to the law, sin and uncleanness were removed by the blood of animal sacrifices. Hence, unusually, this was to be a fountain not only of water but also of blood (see also Moses using water and blood in Heb. 9:19). This is the significance of John's writing of Jesus that 'one of the soldiers pierced his side with a spear, and blood and water flowed out immediately' (John 19:34). Christ's death on the cross is regarded by the evangelist as fulfilling Zechariah's prophecy and providing a fountain for the cleansing of sin and impurity.

It is interesting that this fountain is opened for the king and people living in Jerusalem. Of course, the cleansing effect of Christ's sacrifice on the cross is available to all who will believe (Rev. 7:9, 14); but the death of Christ itself took place exactly here—in Jerusalem, just outside the city gate. Paradoxically the ultimate sin of the rejection of Christ—the Davidic King of Judah—by his own people in Jerusalem became the ultimate source of their forgiveness; and Christ's once and for all offering for sin does away with the need of any further animal sacrifice (Heb. 9:10).

Sin Forsaken

> 13:2 And also on that day," says the LORD who rules over all, "I will remove the names of the idols from the land and they will never again be remembered. Moreover, I will remove the prophets and the unclean spirit from the land.

The cleansing spoken of by the prophet has also a powerful sanctifying effect. Those who are cleansed by the blood of Christ are also set apart for him. They reject idols and turn to God (1 Thess. 1:9) and from all false religious practices; inspired as they are by demons.

There is no more place in God's covenant community for idolatry or falsehood. The people whom he has redeemed by his blood are to be fully committed to a holy God and so are committed to the way of holiness. False religious practices should find no welcome in the church of God, for they will find no welcome in God's presence (Rev. 21:8; 22:15).

Imagine that God would move so mightily on our land, turning so many to Christ, that religious falsehood would be no more able to continue in the nation. Then read this verse again and see that by the proclamation of Christ's cross the dream may become a reality.

> *13:3 Then, if anyone prophesies in spite of this, his father and mother to whom he was born will say to him, 'You cannot live, for you lie in the name of the LORD.' Then his father and mother to whom he was born will run him through with a sword when he prophesies.*

Such an attitude of zero tolerance to sin and rebellion was commonly known to be part of the Mosaic Law. When Jesus later took up this theme he changed it to make it more personal and less violent; yet it became no less severe (Matt. 5:30). The new covenant community (which we now know to be the church) was to have such an uncompromising attitude to sin in their midst that members living in open sin were to be excluded from the community (1 Cor. 5:5).

Sin Frustrated

> *13:4–5 "Therefore, on that day each prophet will be ashamed of his vision when he prophesies and will no longer wear the hairy garment of a prophet to deceive the people. Instead he will say, 'I am no prophet — indeed, I*

> am a farmer, for a man has made me his indentured servant since my youth.'

When God's people are turned to him through his forgiving action, they will pay no more heed to false prophets—thus disenfranchising them and putting them out of business altogether. The picture here is not of the workers of evil being converted, but of them being frustrated. No longer able to deceive the people with their lies, they are humiliated; forced to turn to lowly menial labour to make their living.

> 13:6 And one shall say unto him, What are these wounds in thine hands? Then he shall answer, Those with which I was wounded in the house of my friends (AV).

Still focused on the exegesis of the open fountain, the Shepherd is once again introduced to the narrative. The passage first speaks of his wounding before describing him in more detail. The verse corresponds with that of Psalm 22:16 *'they pierced my hands and feet'*; and describes the nature of Christ's death by crucifixion. Significantly, Jesus describes having received the wounds in the house of his friends – once again pointing to Jerusalem as the place of crucifixion.

> 13:7 "Awake, sword, against my shepherd, against the man who is my associate," says the LORD who rules over all. Strike the shepherd that the flock may be scattered; I will turn my hand against the insignificant ones.

Here God describes the wounded person as 'my companion' or the one who is near to me; words reminiscent of Matthew 3:17, 'This is my beloved son'. The companion is also designated by God as 'my shepherd', the shepherd of my people Israel, a clear Messianic reference (Mic. 5:2). Yet Jesus expanded this ministry to include a flock from all nations when he said, 'And other sheep I have, which are not of this fold: them also I must bring, and they shall hear my voice; and there shall be one fold, and one shepherd' (John 10:16). Hence the writer to the Hebrews describes Christ as 'the great Shepherd of the sheep' (Heb. 13:20).

The awakening sword is a picture of the violence done to the shepherd, upon which the sheep, his disciples (Matt. 26:31), would be scattered.

> *13:8–9 It will happen in all the land, says the LORD, that two-thirds of the people in it will be cut off and die, but one-third will be left in it. Then I will bring the remaining third into the fire; I will refine them like silver is refined and will test them like gold is tested. They will call on my name and I will answer; I will say, 'These are my people,' and they will say, 'The LORD is my God.' "*

These verses initially seem out of place and most likely relate to verse 2, where we first encountered the idea of being 'cut off'. The fate of those who reject God's word and God's shepherd will be to be 'cut off' from God's covenant people; as a result of which exclusion they would perish, not being found justified at the last judgment. The people who are cleansed on the other hand, although spared eternal punishment, will be tried with fire like gold (Job 23:10; 1 Peter 1:7). It is as they share many sufferings because of their testimony that the LORD is their God that they find themselves acknowledged by God as his own people (Acts 14:22; Rom. 8:17).

Discussion Questions for Chapter 13

1. v. 1. In what way can the believer's sin be forgiven?

2. vv. 2–3. Explain how the ideas of forgiveness and sanctification go together in the New Testament, as predicted by Zechariah.

3. vv. 4–9. In what ways does God make a difference between those who respond to his message of cleansing and those who do not?

Chapter 14

The Day of the Lord

> *14:1–2 A day of the LORD is about to come when your possessions will be divided as plunder in your midst. For I will gather all the nations against Jerusalem to wage war; the city will be taken, its houses plundered, and the women raped. Then half of the city will go into exile, but the remainder of the people will not be taken away.*

The day spoken of by Zechariah is a day for the Lord to take action against the nations who oppose Jerusalem. If 'the nations' are seen as the godless of the world, then perhaps Jerusalem is depicted as the only place left on earth being tenaciously faithful to God at a time when all others abandon him (see Ps. 2:1–3). This should always have been the case, but it had not been so in the past, which is why they had been carried into exile. Zechariah's prophecy urges faithfulness in all situations—for even if all nations opposed them, God is the one in whom they must trust.

It may seem strange that a message addressed to those who had just returned from exile after the sacking of Jerusalem by Nebuchadnezzar years earlier should speak of another day when such horrors would be witnessed again. What questions might have arisen in the listeners' minds? Would this happen in their day (the prophet says 'about to come') or at a later time? Was the prophet referring back to an earlier prophecy concerning what had happened under Nebuchadnezzar? Looking back from our modern perspective, are we to understand this prophecy as being fulfilled in the time of the Babylonian invasion, or the Roman destruction of the city, or some other time?

The vital clue which Zechariah gives in answer to these questions is that 'all nations' will be gathered to make war on Jerusalem. Such a universal assault on the holy city has never occurred in history—it is unprecedented. Indeed, never before have 'all nations' gathered against any one country, let alone a single city. What would make the nations of the world consider it necessary to deploy all their combined military might against Jerusalem?

The nature of apocalyptic writings and the meaning of the genre remains a hot topic among scholars. Should such writings be taken symbolically or literally? And if literally, have the visions already been fulfilled, or is their realisation yet to come? These questions are extremely significant in Zechariah 14, which is notoriously difficult to exegete.[20] Personally, I wish both to discuss the rich metaphors which such visions contain (how they relate to God's nature and his purposes for his people) *and also* (cautiously[21]) discuss those aspects of the text which appear to require a literal interpretation. After all, when Daniel saw a vision of four beasts emerging out of the sea, it is clear that he did not envisage a time in the future when awful monsters would rise out of the Mediterranean to destroy the earth! Nevertheless, in years to come, four world powers did arise, just as Daniel predicted; powers which were aptly described by the powerful descriptive metaphors Daniel had employed in his vision.

So then, let us briefly discuss how and when elements of Zechariah's prophecy (14:1-2) might expect a literal fulfilment. The only other passage in scripture where all nations are described as gathering for

---

[20] For a discussion of major approaches, see Al Wolters, 'Zechariah 14: A Dialogue with the History of Interpretation', *MJT* 13 (2002) pp. 39–56

[21] Cautiously, I say, because the future is unfamiliar territory for all of us.

battle near Jerusalem is in the book of Revelation, so that might be a good place to start. In Revelation 16:14–16 all nations gather to the plains of Megiddo for what is popularly called 'the battle of Armageddon'; and in Revelation 19:19 these same armies are depicted as opposing Jesus Christ at the time of his return. Hence in Revelation a reason is proposed for the unity of the nations: they are united by their opposition to Christ and by their seeming awareness that his return to earth is imminent. By comparing the two passages it may reasonably be proposed that Zechariah's prophecy relates to the same period as John's; albeit that it offers a different perspective. If this is so then Zechariah provides important details about this 'end time' conflict which are absent from John's vision. The initial assault of the world's anti-God forces against the city of Jerusalem will be successful, with plunder, rape and exile of many Jews; a statement which ostensibly correlates with Jesus' words in Matthew 24:21–22.

14:3 Then the LORD will go to battle and fight against those nations, just as he fought battles in ancient days.

Whether or not the reader chooses to search for a literal fulfilment of the prophecy, one thing is certain. The reason Zechariah speaks of the trouble of the last days is to introduce his grand theme: the final triumphant appearance of the Lord who brings salvation and vindicates his people. Just as in ancient times—the days when God brought them out of Egypt and into the Promised Land—so God would work in power and glory to redeem his own. Faced with all the problems of their post-exilic period, the Jews could trust in God; for as in the days of Moses they were to again stand still and see the Lord's salvation.

The Apocalyptic vision of God's final triumph over wickedness and the vindication of his people is the blessed hope expected by believers in every era. In days of difficulty, the reminder that good will ultimately conquer evil both sustains faith and provides an incentive for service. This was just the motivation which the returning exiles needed, and which we also need today.

Once again, an interesting correlation is found between this verse and the battle depicted in Revelation, where God's enemies will be destroyed by the word of Christ without a shot being fired (Rev. 19:21); even as in an earlier time Daniel foresaw the forces of evil being destroyed without human hand (Dan. 2:34).

The Lord is Coming to Jerusalem

14:4–5 On that day his feet will stand on the Mount of Olives which lies to the east of Jerusalem, and the Mount of Olives will be split in half from east to west, leaving a great valley. Half the mountain will move northward and the other half southward. Then you will escape through my mountain valley, for the mountains will extend to Azal. Indeed, you will flee as you fled from the earthquake in the days of King Uzziah of Judah. Then the LORD my God will come with all his holy ones with him.

Whether this is a reference to the feet of Christ literally standing on the Mount of Olives (as they certainly did at the time of his ascension); or whether it stands as a metaphor for God's coming near to help his people is not clear. Actually, little can be gained from a 'symbolic' reading of these verses, so perhaps the literal approach will be more fruitful; although in Revelation, when the Lord Jesus Christ is seen to ride out of heaven against his enemies, nothing is said there about his landing on the Mount of Olives. The only reference is to the nearby Mount Zion (Rev. 14:1).

It appears that during the assault on Jerusalem depicted in the opening verses, an earthquake will provide a route of escape for the people of Israel, via a chasm opened through the Mount of Olives. When the Book of Revelation speaks of Jewish suffering at the time of the end, it says 'the earth helped the woman (Israel)' by swallowing an evil 'flood' of persecution (Rev. 12:16). If this passage of Zechariah relates to that same time, then this earthquake provides the means of escape for the remnant of Israel from the wrath of the antichrist and his confederates. As Zechariah and John both indicate, it will be at this time that Christ will appear in the clouds, followed by the armies of heaven, a throng which includes both saints and angels (Rev. 19:11–16; Matt. 16:27).

If we were to examine the powerful metaphors within the verses, then we might see that no matter how desperate the situation, or how dark the night of trouble or persecution (v. 6), God will always come to the aid of his people. The years of exile had been like a dark night for the nation, but God would now arise for their deliverance. For the Christian believer, however, it is impossible to separate the idea of God's final intervention in human affairs from the personal and glorious return of Jesus.

> *14:6 On that day there will be no light — the sources of light in the heavens will congeal.*

As with all apocalyptic writings, even when the events convey a literal meaning, one cannot precisely say whether the events in the vision are concurrent, consecutive, or separated by considerable time. To state the matter simply, if the darkness is literal, when does it take place?

Darkness is a recurring theme in the Bible. In Genesis, it is the state of the world without God's creative activity; for Paul, it represented the state of the human soul without new creation in Christ; and in the Book of Revelation, darkness indicates the coming judgment of God on the earth (Rev. 6:12; 8:12; 9:2) as the necessary prelude to his creation of a new heaven and a new earth. Hence if the darkness of verse six accompanies the coming of 'the LORD my God' to fight against the nations then the picture is one of a dreadful twilight in which God metes out retribution on his enemies.

What is more, that darkness can be seen as indicative both of judgment and as the precursor to new creation is evident from the time when Christ hung on the cross, and the midday sun was turned into midnight darkness which covered the face of the whole earth; Jesus at that time bearing the judgment for sin in order to bring eternal life to humanity.

> *14:7 It will happen in one day (a day known to the LORD); not in the day or the night, but in the evening there will be light.*

If in the previous verse, light became darkness for God's enemies, yet in this verse night becomes day for God's people. As when God brought Israel out of Egypt and provided a pillar of fire by night to light their way, so this light represents the immediate presence of God who descends to act on behalf of his people. Whenever God's people face any kind of trouble, God will be their light and they will never walk in darkness. Eventually, of course, when the sun, moon and stars pass away (Rev. 6:12–14) there will be a new heaven and a new earth (Rev. 21:1) where the Lord will be the only light his people need forever.

> *14:8–10 Moreover, on that day living waters will flow out from Jerusalem, half of them to the eastern sea and half of them to the western sea; it will happen both in summer and in winter. The LORD will then be king over all the earth. In that day the LORD will be seen as one with a single name. All the land will change and become like the Arabah from Geba to Rimmon, south of Jerusalem; and Jerusalem will be raised up and will stay in its own place from the Benjamin Gate to the site of the First Gate and on to the Corner Gate, and from the Tower of Hananel to the royal winepresses.*

In these verses the symbolic nature of the prophecy is predominant; although one ought not to suppose that some kind of literal fulfilment is entirely ruled out. The overall picture of Zechariah's vision is one of God coming to act on behalf of his people against their enemies; and so great is this action that it is described in terms of the movement of the land itself and the changing of the geographical features of a large area around Jerusalem.

With the great earthquake, and the splitting of the Mount of Olives, Jerusalem is raised to a higher altitude above sea level and an underground spring will be released, flowing both east towards the Dead Sea and west toward the Mediterranean. In Ezekiel 47:1–12 we find a similar vision in which the living water brought life and abundant blessing wherever it went, even turning the waters of the Dead Sea fresh so that fish could live there.

The living water flowing from Jerusalem was seen by Jesus as a prophecy concerning the outpouring of the Spirit, which began in Jerusalem at Pentecost, and through which rivers of living water now flow into the hearts of those who believe. The Spirit of God has come to stay, his presence being an abiding taste of future glory, unaffected by seasons or circumstances. However, it was not the Mount of Olives that was riven to set this spring in motion, but Christ himself who was stricken on the cross so that living water might flow from him to all people (to east and west).

The reformers would have seen verses 8–9 as a reference to the word of the Lord going forth from Jerusalem to all nations, bringing men and women under the Lordship of Jesus Christ. *'The LORD will then be king over all the earth. In that day the LORD will be seen as one with a single name.'* Jesus entered into death for every person, but God has highly exalted him and given him the name which is above every name, so that all might bow before him. Jesus has been revealed as the single focal point of worship for men and angels and God has commanded all to bow their knee to him (Heb. 1:6; Phil. 2:9–11).

The place of worship being lifted up (v 10) may also be indicative of this new focal point of worship. Christ becomes of paramount importance, the focus of every area of life. Whatever Christians may do each day, everything is done as unto the Lord; whilst in heaven the Lamb is at the centre of all worship (Rev. 5:8–13).

> *14:11 And men shall dwell therein, and there shall be no more curse; but Jerusalem shall dwell safely. (RV)*

I have chosen the RV as it expresses the thought that there shall be 'no more curse' (as in Rev. 22:3). The redemption which Christ has provided by his death on the cross encompasses the whole of creation (see Rom. 8:21 and Col. 1:20) so that even during his thousand year reign on earth the curse will have been removed; and in the new heaven and earth it will find no place (Rev. 22:3).

God's Enemies Defeated

> *14:12–15 But this will be the nature of the plague with which the LORD will strike all the nations that have fought against Jerusalem: Their flesh will decay while they stand on their feet, their eyes will rot away in their sockets, and their tongues will dissolve in their mouths. On that day there will be great confusion from the LORD among them; they will seize each other and attack one another violently. Moreover, Judah will fight at Jerusalem, and the wealth of all the surrounding nations will be gathered up — gold, silver, and clothing in great abundance. This is the kind of plague that will devastate horses, mules, camels, donkeys, and all the other animals in those camps.*

The realisation that ultimately all of God's enemies will be defeated would have encouraged the defenceless exiles to trust in God for their protection. Once again, if viewed literally, the detail of the prophecy lends itself to the depiction of the battle of Megiddo (Armageddon); since although the manner of the death of the armies that gather at Megiddo to fight against the Lord and his people is not specified in Revelation, it is clearly violent, since the blood of the armies will flow to a depth of at least 1.22 metres for 300 kilometres (Rev. 14:19–20; the width is not specified). Whether or not such figures are accurate, the slaughter is immense (possibly in excess of 100 million persons). Its description calls to my mind eyewitness accounts which I have heard from the victims of the Hiroshima bombing, who saw blood and dead bodies flowing in the river only minutes after the bomb was dropped.

Probably this verse is what inspired the creators of 'Raiders of the Lost Ark' to depict the enemies of God physically melting away, as if caught in the radiation flash of a nuclear explosion. Yet nuclear power is not the cause of death; instead it is the word of Christ (Rev. 19:21). The soldiers' fighting between themselves indicates panic, a futile attempt to get away from the looming judgment. Not only the people but their animals will be destroyed in this manner, and anything of value that remains will become the spoil of war, the property of Israel.

The Feast of Tabernacles

> *14:16 Then all who survive from all the nations that came to attack Jerusalem will go up annually to worship the King, the LORD who rules over all, and to observe the Feast of Tabernacles.*

Without explanation, the prophet announces that there will be survivors of this cataclysmic event, and that they shall come (probably by compunction) to pay homage to the Lord. The observation of the Feast of Tabernacles usually lasted one week, but Zechariah may have the perpetual fulfilment of the Feast of Tabernacles in view. The feast was essentially a thanksgiving for the full harvest, a time of abundance and blessing; and such blessing will become continuous when God comes to dwell among his people (a time defined by many Christians as the Millennium period, where Jesus rules over the earth for one thousand years—Rev. 20:4).

> *14:17–19 But if any of the nations anywhere on earth refuse to go up to Jerusalem to worship the King, the*

> LORD who rules over all, they will get no rain. If the Egyptians will not do so, they will get no rain — instead there will be the kind of plague which the LORD inflicts on any nations that do not go up to celebrate the Feast of Tabernacles. This will be the punishment of Egypt and of all nations that do not go up to celebrate the Feast of Tabernacles.

It is not so much the refusal to attend a feast as the refusal to submit to the Lord that results in punishment; since, during the millennial reign of Christ, he rules with a rod of iron, and enforces the submission of all peoples. Overall the picture is of all nations being compelled to worship the Lord, an image similar to that presented by Paul in Philippians 2:9–11 and 1 Corinthians 15:25–28.

Hence the idea of non-compliance would seem out of place; and the idea of a drought does not fit well with the usual picture of the Millennium: that of reversion to an almost Eden-like state. Likewise, a problem arises since Egypt does not (at present) depend on rain for water; it has the Nile.[22]

Nevertheless the Book of Revelation admits that rebellion will follow the thousand-year reign of Christ. The nations will reveal their true nature as they rebel against the Lord; bringing about their own destruction and the inauguration of the final judgement (Rev. 20:7–15).

> 14:20–21 On that day the bells of the horses will bear the inscription "HOLY TO THE LORD." The cooking pots in the LORD's temple will be as holy as the bowls in front of the

---

[22] Merrill, p. 320

> altar. Every cooking pot in Jerusalem and Judah will become holy in the sight of the LORD who rules over all, so that all who offer sacrifices may come and use some of them to boil their sacrifices in them. On that day there will no longer be a Canaanite in the house of the LORD who rules over all.

The ultimate fulfilment of all eschatological hope is that humankind will dwell in the immediate presence of God, in the restoration of the Eden-type relationship where God walked and talked with people.[23] This hope, for the Christian, is bound up in the person of Christ (Titus 2:13). The sanctification of the articles for temple worship symbolised only a shadow of the reality to come. In the immediate presence of God, everything is hallowed. Even now, since Jesus Christ has been made for us sanctification (1 Cor. 1:30) every word of fellowship, every act of service and every menial task is made holy through Christ. It is his presence that makes them holy; just as God's presence in the bush made the ground beneath Moses' feet holy.

The Canaanite was considered unclean and was not to be admitted to the congregation of the Lord's people. The absence of such people indicates that no one is excluded from the presence of God. All may enter, for the new creation removes all boundaries of race and gender. Just as 'there is neither Jew nor Greek, there is neither slave nor free, there is neither male nor female—for all of you are one in

---

[23] What Craigie calls 'A new sense of God's presence'. Peter C. Craigie, *Twelve Prophets: Micah, Nahum, Habakkuk, Zephaniah, Haggai, Zechariah, and Malachi: Vol. 2* (Edinburgh: Saint Andrews, 1985), p. 221

Christ Jesus' (Gal 3:28),[24] so there are no more Canaanites. They have been made holy through Christ; transformed by new creation.

Discussion Questions for Chapter 14

1. vv. 1–15. In what ways might Zechariah's depiction of God's ultimate victory over all his enemies encourage the returning exiles? In what ways might it comfort God's people today?

2. vv. 4–11. In what ways do you see Zechariah's prophecy as a reference to the second coming of Jesus?

3. vv. 16–21. In what ways might we understand the picture of all nations gathering to worship God to be fulfilled through Jesus?

---

[24] See Merrill p. 320

Bibliography

Assis, Elie, 'Zechariah 8 as Revision and Digest of Zechariah 1–7', *The Journal of Hebrew Scriptures*, Vol. 10 Article 15
<http://www.jhsonline.org/Articles/article_143.pdf>

Baldwin, Joyce G., *Haggai, Zechariah and Malachi* (Leicester: IVP, 1972)

Barker, Margaret, 'The Two Figures in Zechariah', *The Heythrop Journal*, Volume 18, Issue 1, pp. 38–46

Baron, David, *Zechariah: A Commentary on His Visions & Prophecies* (Grand Rapids: Kregel, 1918)

Craigie, Peter C., *Twelve Prophets: Micah, Nahum, Habakkuk, Zephaniah, Haggai, Zechariah, and Malachi: Vol. 2* (Edinburgh: Saint Andrews, 1985)

Hartle, James A., 'The Literary Unity of Zechariah', *The Journal of the Evangelical Theological Society 35/2 (June 1992), pp. 145–157*

Mason, Rex, *The Books of Haggai, Zechariah and Malachi* (Cambridge: University Press, 1977)

Merrill, Eugene H., *Haggai, Zechariah, Malachi: An Exegetical Commentary* (Richardson: Biblical Studies Press, 2013)

Sweeney, Marvin A., *The Twelve Prophets* (Collegeville: Liturgical Press, 2001)

Wolters, Al, 'Zechariah 14: A Dialogue with the History of Interpretation', *Melanesian Journal of Theology* 13 (2002), pp. 39–56